2 156 CER

QM Library

23 1377828 9

KU-113-615

A New History of Medieval French Literature

Rethinking Theory
Stephen G. Nichols and Victor E. Taylor, Series Editors

A New History of Medieval French Literature

JACQUELINE CERQUIGLINI-TOULET

Translated by
SARA PREISIG

The Johns Hopkins University Press

Baltimore

Originally published as "Moyen Âge," in *La littérature française: dynamique et histoire,* edited by Jean-Yves Tadié. © 2007 Éditions Gallimard, Paris.

© 2011 The Johns Hopkins University Press
All rights reserved. Published 2011
Printed in the United States of America on acid-free paper
9 8 7 6 5 4 3 2 1

The Johns Hopkins University Press
2715 North Charles Street
Baltimore, Maryland 21218-4363
www.press.jhu.edu

Library of Congress Cataloging-in-Publication Data

Cerquiglini-Toulet, Jacqueline.
 A new history of medieval French literature / Jacqueline Cerquiglini-Toulet.
  p.   cm.
 Includes bibliographical references and index.
 ISBN-13: 978-1-4214-0303-8 (hardcover : acid-free paper)
 ISBN-10: 1-4214-0303-X (hardcover : acid-free paper)
  1. French literature—To 1500—History and criticism. I. Title.
 PQ156.C47 2011
 840.9'001—dc22   2011011228

A catalog record for this book is available from the British Library.

Special discounts are available for bulk purchases of this book. For more information, please contact Special Sales at 410-516-6936 or specialsales@press.jhu.edu.

The Johns Hopkins University Press uses environmentally friendly book materials, including recycled text paper that is composed of at least 30 percent post-consumer waste, whenever possible.

CONTENTS

TRANSLATOR'S NOTE

In translating the present work, I have attempted to stay close to the original text while giving it an American style. For the major works cited by Jacqueline Cerquiglini-Toulet, I have used existing translations, which are included in the bibliography. For the other numerous texts quoted throughout this work, I have supplied my own translations.

I would like to thank Yvonne Lucero and Peter Dreyer for their invaluable proofreading and stylistic suggestions as well as Florian Preisig, who gave up much of his own research time to tirelessly read and reread this translation for content as well as form. Any remaining typographical or stylistic errors fall directly to me.

A New History of Medieval French Literature

Introduction

Medieval Literature?

Does it make sense to write a history of the French literature of the Middle Ages? Strictly speaking, no. Meanings of words have changed, including that of the word *littérature*; in Old French, *literature* refers to Latin literature. This is the case for the oldest attested use of the term, which is found in Philippe de Thaon's twelfth-century Bestiary, ll. 955–956, where we read, "Judeus literature/Tant entant d'escripture" (The Jew understands the letter of literature so well). Philippe's point is to contrast literal meaning, *escripture*, with allegorical meaning. In other words, the Jew reads texts literally but does not understand their allegorical meaning. But the word surprised at least one scribe: another manuscript gives for line 955, "the traitorous Jew" (*Judeus, li traiture*), coming back to a commonplace that does not correspond to the context.

The word *literature* does not seem to be used with the meaning that we give it today until the end of the Middle Ages, the very end. In his *Séjour d'Honneur*, composed between 1489 and 1494, Octovien de Saint-Gelais speaks of René of Anjou as an "expert poet, loving literature" (*poëthe expert, aymant licterature*). Given the prince's tastes, *licterature* cannot possibly refer solely to the Classics here. However, in 1513 when Jean Lemaire de Belges, in his conclusion to *Les Illustrations de Gaule et Singularitez de Troye*, addresses his male readers as "noble men and experts in literature," he is indeed still referring to the Classics. A second caveat is tied to the role that orality plays in the production of literature and in the way in which it is transmitted; not by written text but by voice. Must we then accept the practice of putting the phrase "medieval French literature" in quotations marks? No: a literary awareness did exist in the Middle Ages, as I intend to show in the following chapters. In so doing, I shall also attempt to answer, indirectly and modestly, the ambitious question: "What is literature?"

What place has been given to the Middle Ages in general literary histories since the turning point in historical criticism? Their place is not insignificant in Gustave de Lanson's *Histoire de la littérature française,* the first edition of which, dated 1894, marks the beginning of the genre. But, in the case of the Middle Ages, it is in fact a question of judgments, mostly negative, that convey a series of a priori about broad categories: peoples or women, for example. Thus Chrétien de Troyes is a "man from Champagne who is sensible and happy to live . . . the man the least capable of understanding what he was recounting" (champenois avisé et content de vivre . . . l'homme le moins fait pour comprendre ce qu'il contait); Christine de Pizan, the first of an "intolerable lineage of women-authors" (insupportable lignée de femmes-auteurs). On the other hand, the Middle Ages are discussed by specialists in *Histoire de la langue et de la littérature française des origines à 1900,* published in 1896 under the direction of Louis Petit de Julleville. Two out of eight volumes, one fourth of the collection, are dedicated to the Middle Ages, and of the ten collaborators, six were students of Gaston Paris, the master in this field of study. The perspective is that of a history of genres, and this well-established approach endures.

This will not be my choice of presentation insofar as the genre, thus conceived—lyricism, romance, theater—or more generally speaking: epic, lyric, dramatic, is a normative category that one could apply to all literature whatever its conditions of realization. Even if this approach facilitates description, it creates false problems and responds to questions that are not even asked. Closer to us, if we examine the various tendencies that have appeared in the history of medieval literature, two sizable trends can be discerned: the one followed by those, like Curtius, who work at showing a continuity, from Antiquity to the modern era; and the trend of those who, like Hans Robert Jauss, insist on the discontinuity and, consequently, on the otherness of the Middle Ages.

The historical gap that separates us from the Middle Ages is obvious. But what can we do about it? Fill it in, by looking for what connects us to those centuries: tradition, memory? Glorify it, by making the Middle Ages into an anthropological object? "Alterity and Modernity," the binomial that Jauss concentrated on in the 1970s, summarized by Paul Zumthor in *Parler du Moyen Age*:

> A radical duplicity that (if we follow Hans Robert Jauss) is the foundation of the very interest and, for us, the benefit of medieval studies: observation of the alterity of the Middle Ages (definable both along the lines of duration and at the level of the structures) provokes in us the perception of an identity of which it reveals the components.

This approach offers an understanding of what we are through the perception of what the other was.

It may be a question of another alterity as well. In collecting a selection of his essays under the title *Pour un autre Moyen Age* (For Another Middle Ages), Jacques Le Goff sought to refute a trompe l'oeil vision of the Middle Ages, built on preconceived ideas, conscious or not: the gloomy Middle Ages of the Romantics, the bright Middle Ages of Gustave Cohen or Régine Pernoud. Playing on the use that our era makes of the term "Middle Ages" with reference to an apocalyptic future, Umberto Eco entitled one of his articles for *L'Espresso* "Il Nuovo Medioevo" (The New Middle Ages)[1] which, in turn, enabled him to compare these fantasized uses of the word with some essential categories of medieval thought.

Mixed in with the notion of alterity are the questions of invariants and variables, and of diversity and proximity—the same and the other. This study will be sensitive to the conceptual horizon on which the works that have come down to us today stand out, and sensitive also to the reflection, most often indirect, on the forms and styles that the Middle Ages provoke. The word "genre" is used here in this sense. I do not graph the rises and falls of a literature that emerges, blooms, and declines, on a vitalist model. Neither do I offer an account imitating those of periods and reigns, the latter term, for that matter, not being entirely pertinent to the Middle Ages. My ambition is to define a history of the concepts that allow us to account for the literary production of four or five centuries, concepts grasped in their medieval use and in their amplitude. I am aiming at a history of the literary act, a history of words, in a way, that measures the difference of thoughts on literature in the Middle Ages and today: for time is registered in words, as in bodies. This can also be seen as a history of ideas and works, monuments rather than documents, that questions us about our concept of literature: the Middle Ages as a heuristic tool for thinking about literature.

To achieve this, we must maintain the feeling of mild strangeness that this language, our language, procures for us; and you, the reader, must be willing to understand it in a graphic form that may occasionally be disconcerting. This is the price of giving a new sense to words, enjoying their discovery and their taste, and making ancient literature play out as a practice of knowledge and pleasure.

It All Began Like This

The question of origins haunted reflections on medieval literature throughout the nineteenth and a good part of the twentieth centuries. Scholars sought the origins of the *chanson de geste*, the origins of lyrical poetry. For the *chansons de geste*, one particular turn of phrase, taken from the French medieval historian Joseph Bédier [1864–1938], has been highly influential: "In the beginning was the [pilgrimage] road." Rejecting the existing theory of a continuity of development from the event to the poem, for example, from the battle of Roncevaux to the Oxford manuscript version of the *Chanson de Roland*, Bédier saw the birth of the *chanson de geste* in the legends linked to the churches on the pilgrimage routes. This first turn of phrase led to a second: "In the beginning was the poet," an affirmation of an individual creation of these texts. Others, however, took up the banner "In the beginning was the voice." Today, faced with texts that for us are written, we affirm: in the beginning was language, French, a young language, a new language. What was attempted with this material? Maurice Maeterlinck uses a striking image in his preface to the French translation of the fourteenth-century *Spiritual Espousals* [originally in Flemish] by the Blessed Jan van Ruusbroec [1293?–1381]: "Words are really lamps behind ideas," and he continues: "I am also disposed to believe that every language thinks always more than the man, even the man of genius, who employs it, and who is only its heart for the time being."[2]

At the heart of a Latin chronicle, the *Sacramenta Argentariae* (Oaths of Strasbourg) [between the Carolingian-Frankish rulers Louis the German and Charles the Bald], dating from the year 842, simultaneously an event, a document, and a monument, we find the first written evidence of the French and Germanic languages. The text has a factual importance and also a quasi-mythical one in the imaginary over the centuries, to such an extent that, from this alone, one could write a history of the histories of French literature and language, from Jean Bodin to Raymond Queneau. French in the heart of Latin, this is the situation of the French language and literature in the Middle Ages.

LATIN-FRENCH BILINGUALISM

Fundamentally, the Middle Ages is a period of Latin-French bilingualism that distinguishes two cultures: a learned culture of those who master Latin, the clerics, and a culture of laymen. Included in this uneducated ensemble, of course, are the *illiterati*, not only the people but also the greater part of the noble class. Latin represents authority, the authority of the liturgy, of knowledge, and of power. The language of the schools and universities, it is sometimes simply called "grammar," the first of the liberal arts. It is in these terms that many authors of the twelfth century write in French about their Latin source: the book of grammar, for example, from which Philippe de Thaon, one of the first to write scientific literature in the vernacular language, says he has taken his *Bestiary* and a *Lapidary*. A language that is not accessible to all, Latin reinforces its power with its obscurity. The word *grammaire* in Old French has a variant *grimoire* [book of magic spells], which underlines the occult side and the relationship of Latin to the written text.

For the clerics, however, Latin abolishes boundaries; it is the language of intercomprehension. Jacques Legrand, in the fourteenth century, underscores this in the chapter *"Gramaire"* of his *Archiloge Sophie*: "This language is propitious for conversing together when the spoken language of one another is not the same." The case of Laurent de Premierfait, translator of Boccaccio's *Decameron*, is significant. He explains in his prologue that he did not translate the text directly from Florentine but worked through Latin, thanks to a friar "a very good man who knew vulgar Florentine and the Latin language." Latin remains at the center of communication for the clerics. It can play a role that seems very strange, from our point of view, in the channels of communication. A scene from a thirteenth-century Arthurian romance, *Gliglois*, gives an idea of the complex transactions that were played out between the written and the oral, and between Latin and vernacular. The heroine, Beauty, wants to send a letter to her sister. She has it written by a monk, "telling" him "the matter," says the text, and he writes it in Latin: "He memorized it and wrote it in Latin on parchment" (Cil la retint et en latin l'a escript ens el parchemin). A complex circuit that goes from the vernacular or vulgar speech of a female character to a monk's memory and from there to the transcription of this memorized word into Latin. As if Latin alone, by its nobility, justifies being written down.

At the other end of the chain, the sister of the lady will have the letter read to her by a chaplain who, therefore, reads Latin and translates it into French for his listener. Memory plays a capital role in this transmission. The transmission is translation.

OC AND OÏL, LANGUAGES AND DIALECTS

The territory of the Gauls is divided by two languages of Latin origin, named for the way they affirm something: the way they say yes. In the north there is the *langue d'oïl* and in the south, the *langue d'oc*. Dante gives an account of this and includes his own language, the language of *sì*, in the *De vulgari eloquentia* (On Eloquence in the Vernacular). But the linguistic richness is much greater still. Languages not derived from Latin also meet on the territory of what will become France: Flemish, Breton. And this diversity is thought of in terms of wealth. Such is the feeling of Etienne de Conty in his *Brevis tractatus*. The status of dialects, however, is more complex, bringing to life feelings of superiority or of inferiority. Chrétien de Troyes evokes, at the beginning of the *Knight of the Cart*, "a great number of beautiful courtly ladies, skillful at conversing in French" (Mainte bele dame cortoise/Bien parlant en lengue françoise). He is referring to the superiority of a level of language, that of the courts, sort of an illustrious vernacular, such as Dante would give us to understand. This reflects a sentiment of superiority for the French spoken in Ile-de-France when its speakers find themselves confronted with the French spoken in England since the Norman Conquest. "My language is good, for I was born in France" (Mis langages est bons, car en France fui nez), writes Guernes de Pont-Sainte-Maxence—who is in England—in his *Vie de saint Thomas Beckett* (1173). Coming from the opposite direction, numerous authors—some of them born of Breton mothers—apologize for their language using the formula "For I was not born in Paris" (Car nés ne suis pas de Paris). "Because my mother was a pure Breton" (Car ma mere estoit pure Brete), Olivier de la Haye pleads in a 1426 poem about the Black Death of 1348; my "nourishing language first came from the country of Savoy" (langue nutritive/Partit premier du pays de Savoye), Jacques de Bugnin declares in his *Congié pris du siècle seculier* (1480). The variant that Jean Baudouin, from Lorraine, uses in the fifteenth century unites language with historic and dynastic memory: "I was not born in Saint-Denis in France" (né ne fu mie de Saint Denis en France). A nun from Barking (is it Clémence?) warns the reader in her *Vie d'Edouard le Confesseur*: "I know a false French from England, for I did not go elsewhere to find it" (Un faus franceis sai d'Angleterre/Ke ne l'alai ailurs quere). She asks the reader, then, to amend her language where he finds it necessary. Henry of Lancaster does likewise in his *Livre des Saintes Médecines* (Book of Holy Medicines): "And if the French were not good, I must be excused for this because I am English and have not frequented French very much" (si le franceis ne soit pas bon, jeo doie estre escusee, pur ceo qe jeo sui engleis et n'ai pas moelt hauntee le franceis). Others, who are conscious of their rank and of the value of their language, protest. For instance, Conon de Béthune, in one of his songs, complains about the way in which the queen, mother of the young Philip II Augustus, laughed at his Picardy dialect: "They are neither well educated nor courteous, those who corrected me if I used Artesian words, for I was not raised in Pontoise" (Ne chil ne sont bien apris ne cortois,/S'il m'ont repris se j'ai dis mos d'Artois,/Car je ne fui pas norris a Pontoise).

LITERARY LANGUAGE AND GENRES

An important point emerges from this feeling toward language: the awareness of an affinity between certain languages or certain dialects and specific literary matters. Raimon Vidal de Basalù expresses this in his *Razos de trobar*. The French language is more apt and better suited to the composition of *romans* and *pastourelles*; the "limousi" (the language of the troubadours) to the composition of *vers e cansos e sirventes*, that is to say, stanzas, love songs, and satirical poems. Dante develops the same concept in his *De vulgari eloquentia*: "Thus the language of *oïl* adduces on its own behalf the fact that, because of the greater facility and pleasing quality of its vernacular style, everything that is recounted or invented in vernacular prose belongs to it: such as compilations from the Bible and the gestes of Troy and Rome, and the beautiful tales of King Arthur (*Arturi regis ambages pulcerrime*), and many other works of history and doctrine. The second part, the language of *oc*, argues in its own favor that eloquent writers in the vernacular first composed poems in this sweeter and more perfect language." Others find themselves being criticized for writing of noble subjects in vernacular. Thus, the author of *Partonopeu de Blois* writes: "These clerics say that it is not wise for me to write an ancient history insofar as I am not writing it in Latin and that in the end I am wasting my time" (Cil clerc dient que n'est pas sens/Qu'es[c]rive estoire d'antif tens/Quant jo nes escris en latin,/Et que je perç mon tans en fin; ll. 77–80).

Others hold themselves back from writing more before certain scientific developments in French occur. Such is the case of Evrart de Conty when he writes about the seven types of mirrors in his *Livre des eschez amoureux moralisés*: "But we will put aside the great subtleties and the powerful demonstrations that are not well adapted to French" (Maiz nous lairons les grans soutilletés et les demonstracions fortes qui ne sont pas bien seans en françois).

A good example of the impact of language on literary genres is the shift that is noticeable during this period, from the word *Romance* as language to the word *romance* as a category of writing. *Roman* (romance) in *Roman de Renart* refers to stories by Renart written in *langue romane* (Romance language). At this point, we find ourselves in a situation that distinguishes these texts from those in Latin, from the *Ysengrimus*, for example. However, when Chrétien speaks of his *Cligès* as a *romance*, compared to the *tale*, taken from the *book* that he claims to have found in the library of the church of Saint-Pierre in Beauvais, he is referring to a mode of narration. And the development of this mode of narration is one of the characteristics of this form of literature in French. As for the *langue d'oc*, the language of southern France, it carries a considerable weight in the writings of love. The reputation of the people of Provence is well established in this domain. As early as the thirteenth century, Philippe Mousket asserts this in his chronicle (ll. 6301–6302), "The Provençals make better songs and melodies than the people of other countries" (Font Provenciel et cans et sons/Millors que gent d'autre païs), and he reinforces this statement with a genealogical explanation: when Charlemagne divided his conquests, he supposedly gave Provence in fief to the minstrels and jongleurs who had followed his army. Poetry is passed down, in a way, with the land; the Provençals are poets "by nature" (l. 6300). The reputation of Poitou, in *langue d'oc* territory, is particularly strong. John of Salisbury, who wrote his *Policraticus* [1159?] in Latin, speaks to his book as if it were a pilgrim: "Leave and, wherever you go, say that you were born in Poitou, for they have permission to speak a more frank language."[3] The political reasons behind this preeminence are obvious: Poitiers is a fief of the Plantagenets and Eleanore of Aquitaine holds an important court there. Poitiers' reputation, moreover, is ambivalent in the Middle Ages. To be "born in Poitou" (*Poitou nez*)—we can find this wording used by Henri d'Andeli—is a way of indicating deception. Isn't the etymology of *Poitiers*, for John of Salisbury, "the painted bird" (*l'oysel paint*), the magpie, a bird of questionable reputation? "Cheating in Poitiers is Justice, Lady and Viscountess" (Tricherie est en Poitou/Justice, Dame et Viscontesse), affirms Raoul de Houdenc in his *Songe d'Enfer* (Dream of Hell). This does not stop the *sons poitevins* (Songs from Poitou) from being renowned and often cited in the jongleurs' repertoire. In the epic poem *Les Quatre fils Aymon*, two of the brothers, Alart and Guichart, strike up "a song" (*.I. son*). The text specifies that "the words were in Gascon, the melody in Limousin" (Gasconois fu li dis et limosins li ton; l. 6600). Language intertwines with love in poetry; it also intertwines with politics.

LANGUAGE AND POWER

Outside of France, French is perceived as a cultural language. This is the case in Italy. Brunetto Latini gives two reasons for writing his *Book of the Treasure* in French although he is Italian: one factual reason, "because I am in France," and one aesthetic and symbolic reason, "because the spoken language is more delightful and is more common to all languages" (por çou que la parleure est plus delitable et plus commune a tous langages) or to "all people" (*toutes gens*) according to other manuscripts. Delightful (*delitable*) and common (*commun*) French is used by Martin da Canal who writes his *Estoires de Venise* (Stories of Venice) in French, most probably between 1267 and 1275. He puts forward the same rea sons as Brunetto Latini: "The French language is shared by the world and is more delightful to read and to hear than any other" (lengue franceise cort parmi le monde et est plus delitable a lire et a oïr que nule autre). Doesn't it say in *The Golden Legend* that Saint Francis received from God the gift of the French language and that "still, when he was ablaze with the fire of the Holy Spirit, he expressed his burning emotions in French" (toujours, quand il était embrasé du feu de l'Esprit-Saint, il exprimait en français ses émotions brûlantes)? Thus emerges in the north of Italy in the fourteenth century a literary dialect, Franco-Italian, in which Niccolò da Verona, for example, writes his *Pharsale*. In the Latin kingdoms of the East [Cyprus and Jerusalem], even Italians wrote in French, as exemplified by [the Lombard] Philippe de Novare's *Des quatre tenz d'aage d'ome* [ca 1265].

The relationship in England between the French language and power is obvious. The language of the conqueror, it is spoken at court until the fourteenth century; even if the children have to be forced to learn it. There is the feeling of a hierarchy of languages, placing French, "the language of the angels," just under Latin, "the language of God." But the French-English war, in the fourteenth century, exacerbates the rivalry between the languages and the retreat of French is notable, even if authors such as Geoffrey Chaucer and John Gower continue to write in the three languages: Latin, English, and French. John Gower, at the end of his *Traictié selonc les auctours pour essampler les amantz marietz* (Treaty for the Authors to Serve as an Example to Married Lovers) signals, in spite of everything: "And if I do not have the abundance of speech of the French, excuse me if in this I err: I am English" (Et si jeo n'ai de François la faconde / Pardonetz moi qe jeo de ceco forsvoie: / Jeo sui Englois). We can see, going in the same direction, a trend toward translation of French romances from previous centuries into English. This is the case, for example, of *Guillaume de Palerne*, translated into English circa 1350. Similarly, after the Albigensian crusade, a gap appears between *langue d'oïl* and *langue d'oc*. The anonymous author of the novella *Frayre de Joy et Sor de Plaser* (Brother of Joy and Sister of Pleasure) bears witness to this. He opens his text with these remarks: "Although the French have a beautiful language, I do not like their lineage at all, for they are ruthlessly proud . . . this is why I do not wish to speak French" (Bien que les

Français aient un beau langage, je n'aime en rien leur lignage, car ils sont orgueilleux sans merci . . . c'est pourquoi je ne veux pas parler français).

THE QUESTION OF THE SPOKEN WORD

We deal with medieval texts in writing, but we well know that prior to these texts there were, for a certain number of them, oral accounts, a circulation of legends: that speech accompanied the written word in the transmission of messages, as well as the texts in their recitation in the public square or in the courts. An immense, lost, continent of voices. Voices before and after the texts: Church chants—the *Séquence de sainte Eulalie*, Church-related chants—the *Chanson de sainte Foy d'Agen*, cantilenas, epic poems, troubadours' songs. In the prologue to her *Lays*, Marie de France describes the different choices she has before her with regards to her writing. Either "to compose some good story and pass it from Latin to French" (Aucune bone estoire faire/Et de latin en romaunz traire), but, she says, others have already done that, or "to compose" (*faire ditié*), to make a poetic work from the lays that she has heard sung and that she chooses to put in writing. She insists on the verb "to hear" (*oïr*). In both cases, it is a question of translation, of a transfer: into *roman*, into a Romance language, in the first, and into writing in the second. Who sang? Jongleurs, Breton jongleurs: "[the tales] from which the Bretons took their lays" (Dunt li Bretun unt fait les lais) she says at the opening of *Guigemar*, or the elderly: "the elders made a lay" (Firent un lai li auncïen), as she specifies at the conclusion of the lay *Milun*, underlining her role "and I who have put it into writing take great pleasure in telling it" (Et jeo, ki l'ai mis en escrit,/Al recunter mut me delit). The elders belong to two types of sources for Marie de France: the great authors of the Antiquity, to whom she alludes in her general prologue, and the aged, whose memory should be treasured. It is again to the memory of these aged, "the good old people who know it by heart" (les bons vieillardz qui en sçavent par cueur), that Clément Marot appeals when attempting to restore the corrupted text by François Villon in his 1533 edition. This combination makes up a double culture that is characteristic of the medieval world in the vernacular.

Certain traits of medieval writing must be considered in relation to this intimate tie to the voice. Such as the absence or the rarity of any punctuation in the manuscripts: what is more, punctuation, when it does exist, is purely rhythmic. Theodor Adorno rightly affirms in his reflection on punctuation marks, in "On the Use of Foreign Words," that they "bring writing to resemble the voice." The medieval manuscript, which is closely linked to the voice, does not need them. This aspect of medieval literature is covered remarkably well by Paul Zumthor in his work *La Lettre et la voix*. The investigation is fed by the research of anthropologists, ethnologists, and folklorists. What we can retain from these reflections for our purpose is the carnal dimension of texts that are, indeed, an embodied speech. It is, after all, the other side of the coin that we will question: writing. The term actually seems to be the same used by medieval language to designate, in French, *belles-lettres*, that which we call "literature." "For tell us a story, either a song or an adventure" (Car nos dites une escriture/o de chançon o d'aventure; ll. 129–130) the host requests of the *povre clerc* (poor cleric) that he is housing, in the fabliau of the same name. "Dire une écriture" truly seems to mean "say a literary text," even if the tale that the cleric tells is, in the form of a fable, the recounting of his own adventure. It is this same term "*écriture*" (writing) that Clément Marot uses in the preface of his edition of Villon. He is pleased that time has not erased the poet's oeuvre and adds: "And even less will it be erased now and henceforth, being that good French writings are and will be better known and collected than ever" (Et moins encor l'effacera ores et d'icy en avant, que les bonnes escriptures françoises sont et seront myeulx congneues et recueillies que jamais).

PART ONE

Writing in the Middle Ages

What is needed to write a book? Jean Froissart tells us in the opening of his *Joli Buisson de Jonece*: "Sense and memory, ink and paper and writing case, penknife and sharpened quill, and ready will" (Sens et memore/Encre et papier et escriptore,/Kanivet et penne taillie,/Et volenté apparellie; ll. 3–6), that is, three types of tools: intellectual qualities: sense and memory; instruments that come under the category of the materiality of writing: the ink, the paper, the writing case, the little penknife for removing errors, the finely sharpened quill; and the will to write. Thus, we must begin with three investigations. They will concentrate on the abovementioned material conditions for writing, on the question of the author, and finally on the relationship between the notion of will and its silent partner or, in a broader sense, its audience.

CHAPTER ONE

The Materiality of Writing

Ｉｎ　ｔｈｅ　ｍｉｄｄｌｅ　ａｇｅｓ, books were manuscripts: the handwritten codices that made their appearance in the fourth century CE and whose use drastically changed the relationship to culture. A few scrolls (the Latin word is *volumen*) subsisted in the medieval era, but for very specific types of texts: scrolls of chronicles, scrolls recording deaths or for short pieces: songs, scrolls on which prayers or magical formulae were written, spells, theater *rollets* that at times contain only one actor's lines. A few particular cases have given rise to questions, such as the *Evangile aux femmes*, a satirical text, found both in numerous codices and on a single scroll. Manuscripts were produced by scribes, often assembled in scriptoria, originally monastic, then secular. In the Middle Ages, a scribe was called an *escrivain*; this is the first sense of the word and was for a long time—until the thirteenth century—its only meaning in Old French.[1] Some names of scribes are known. Perhaps the most famous for his connection to the literary work is Guiot, who copied Chrétien de Troyes' *romans* a century after their composition in what is now French National Library, *fonds français* (BNF, fr.) manuscript 794. At the conclusion of *Yvain*, he notes: "This manuscript was copied by Guiot" (Cil qui l'escrist Guioz a non). This colophon also gives the permanent location of his workshop in Provins [Seine-et-Marne], "before the church of Our Lady of the Valley" (devant Nostre Dame del Val/est ses osteus tot a estal). Jean Madot signed his transcription of the *Roman de Troie* (manuscript BNF, fr. 375), priding himself on being the nephew of Adam de la Halle. He also gives the date of his copy: Candlemas 1288. Other scribes are attached to an important personage. Thus Raoul Tainguy, whose writing is so distinctive, often signs the manuscripts that he copies with his name or with the mention *le caterval*, the good drunkard, equivalent to a signature. He seems to have been the appointed *escrivain* of Arnaud de Corbie, a man of power in the Armagnac party, chancellor of France between 1388 and

1413. He copied Eustache Deschamps' "complete" works, manuscript BNF, fr. 840, for de Corbie.

Writing is work and art. As early as the eighth century, a scribe enjoys underlining the tiresome side of this work through a word game that recalls rhymes and riddles (*formulettes et devinettes*): "Tres digiti scribunt, duo oculi vident. Una lingua loquitur, totum corpus laborat": three fingers, two eyes, one tongue, an enumeration in decrescendo that culminates in the totality of the body. *Le Livre de Sidrac*, from the end of the thirteenth century, similarly declares: "He who writes makes his whole body suffer, his eyes, his brain, and his kidneys, and he dares neither think nor look nor laugh nor speak nor hear nor listen; he doesn't dare think of anything except that which he is writing, and he who does not know how to write cannot imagine that writing is an art" (Qui escrit, il travaille tout son cors et les ielz et la cervelle et les rains, si n'ose penser ne regarder ne rire ne parler ne oïr ne escouter mais que en son escrivre, et qui ne set escrivre ne cuide que l'escripture soit art).

In his *Description de la ville de Paris au XVe siècle* (Description of the City of Paris in the Year 1407), Guillebert de Metz calls attention to the fame of Paris copyists, singling out "the sovereign scribe Gobert, who improved the art of writing and of sharpening quills; and his pupils, such as the duc de Berry's young Flamel, who were retained by princes because of their good writing" (Item Gobert, le souverain escripvain, qui composa l'Art d'escripre et de taillier plumes; et ses disciples qui par leur bien escripre furent retenus des princes, comme le juenne Flamel du duc de Berry).

To encourage his scribes, Jean Gerson wrote a treatise for them singing their praises: *De laude scriptorum* (In Praise of Scribes). But scribes could also have a bad reputation. They might deceive out of greed, as is pointed out in *La Somme le Roi*: "like these writers who show good writing in the beginning and then do it poorly" (comme cil escrivain qui montrent bone letre au commencement et puis la font mauvaise). They may be stupid, even lazy. Such is the opinion of Petrarch who, in one of his letters to Boccaccio, writes: "They have the habit, indeed, a strange thing, of writing not what they are given to copy, but something, I don't know what, that is anything but that, they are so filled with ignorance, laziness or disdain" (Ils ont coutume, en effet, chose étrange, d'écrire non ce qu'on leur donne à copier, mais je ne sais quoi qui est tout autre, tant il y a en eux d'ignorance, de paresse ou de mépris).

This sentiment signals the new relationship of the author to his text, which he did not want to see altered. The concern or desire to control is such that they sometimes push the poet to become his own scribe. Thus Petrarch copied his *Rerum vulgarium fragmenta* (Latin Vatican manuscript 3195). Along the same lines, in England we have holograph manuscripts by Thomas Hoccleve.

A specific demon lies in wait for professional scribes: Titivillus. He intervenes in the errors that come from the oral as well as the written tradition, keeping track of syllables dropped from prayers or the psalmody out of haste and of words skipped or altered in copying. He collects these—written matter whose burden is also moral—in a big bag in order to weigh them on Judgment Day.

The material of the manuscript is parchment. Paper was not to be found in France until the middle of the thirteenth century. One of the first appearances of the word in French is in Guillaume de Machaut's *Voir-dit*, where the poet says to his secretary: "Take some paper, I want to write" (Pren dou papier, je veuil escrire; l. 3045). But other materials exist: materially speaking, wax tablets; metaphorically, the heart, memory. Just as for the act of writing, riddles use wax tablets as their object:

Demande
Par engien fut fait vaisseau de fust; de cire moult est biau,
et vuit et plain tout d'un poiz est; adevinez que c'est.

Response
C'est ung tableau de cyre a escripre de greffe.

LES ADEVINEAUX AMOUREUX, NO. 501

(*Question*: By subtle art, a wooden recipient was made; wax makes it beautiful; empty or full, it has the same weight; guess what it is. *Answer*: It is a wax tablet upon which one writes with a stylet.)

Texts evoke every aspect of the concrete act of composing. The author creates a song in his memory. He teaches it orally to his messenger, who transmits it: "Without a letter on parchment, I send this poem, that we sing in simple Romance language, to Uc le Brun, by Filhol" (Senes breu de parguamina: Tramet lo vers, que chantam/En plena lengua romana,/A.n Hugo Bru per Filhol), says Jaufré Rudel. We encounter a similar insistence in a message "without a charter sealed with wax, without a parchment and without a skin of lower quality" (sanz chartre seëllee en cire,/sanz parchemin et sanz alue) in the *Roman de la Poire* (ll. 839–840). Guillaume de Machaut's fourteenth-century *Voir-dit* offers a staged production of the different moments of the intellectual composition of a poem and of its material copy. The poet composes a ballad. Does he sing it? The text does not specify. The lady then asks to see it: "So that her mouth could read it, for, in the event that she did read it, she would understand it much better" (Par quoi sa bouche la leüst,/Car, en cas qu'elle la liroit,/Assez mieulz l'en entenderoit; ll. 2365–2367). (Note that one reads with one's mouth, murmuring, articulating.) While the poet's scribe (*escrivain*) is copying the ballad, the lady reads it, "in such a way that she knew a part of it before her departure" (Si qu'elle en sot une partie/Ains que de la fust departie; ll. 2373–2374). The text is once again entrusted to an immaterial support: memory.

What are the consequences of such modes of transmission? We possess few handwritten manuscripts from ancient eras and even fewer rough drafts, wax tablets having undoubtedly served this purpose. In spite of everything, certain hands have been identified, Christine de Pizan's in particular, and a few rough drafts have been preserved. The same is true of Giraud de Barri, Baudouin Butor, and Georges d'Esclavonie. The case of Baudouin Butor is particularly significant. He left four rough drafts of an Arthurian romance in prose copied in the margins and unused spaces of a manuscript compilation dated 1294 that no doubt belonged to him. This is the draft of a rewriting of a *Merlin*, known under the name of *Roman des fils du roi Constant* or *Roman de Pandragus et Libanor*. In the rondeau that ends her *Epistre à la Reine* in manuscript BNF, fr. 580, Christine de Pizan confides the circumstances of the work's composition, underlining her devotion with the mention that she worked into the late hours of the night and without the help of a scribe.

> Prenez en gré s'il vous plaist, cest escript
> De ma main fait apres mienuit une heure.

> (Be so kind as to accept, please, this writing done by my hand at one in the morning.)

But, as she points out to her addressee:

Quand vous plaira, mieulz vous sera rescript,
Mais n'avoye nul autre clerc à l'eure.

(If it pleases you, it will be better copied for you, but I had no scribe at the time.)

The calligraphy of the work is a type of edition. The materiality of the manuscript—the skin of the animal that was used to make it—plays a large role in the imagination. The book that we want to criticize is brought back to the skin that it is made of. The villein in Jean Dupin's *Mélancolies* sees in Holy Scripture only the materiality of the skins that it is written upon: "Do you have faith, says he, in this skin?" (Creez, fait il, en celle peaulx? l. 2529). The author of the *Somme le Roi*, to abbreviate one of the subcategories of his chapter on Avarice, recalls: "each can better read these sins [that is, those that stem from avarice] and the others in the book of his heart than on sheepskin" (miex puet chascuns ces pechés et les autres lire en livre de son cuer que en la pel de barbix). Playing on his name—*fèvre* meant "smith" in old French—Jean Le Fèvre concludes his *Livre de Leesce* (Book of Joy) with these words: "For he does not know how to work with iron but gives all his care to skins" (Car il ne scet ouvrer en fer,/mais en peaulx est toute sa cure; ll. 3978–3979).

At times, the boundary between scribe and author is blurred, the same person playing both roles. In particular, this was the case with monks who dedicated themselves to the work of copying but could also compose pieces in their own names. Matthieu Paris (c. 1200–1259) copied and illuminated his Latin and Anglo-Norman works. Guillaume Alexis, who signed copies of some of the manuscripts of his abbey at Lyre [in Haute-Normandie], was an author who would also succeed in print. Jean Joret, official scribe of Kings Charles VII and Louis XI, dedicated a poem of his own making about the alphabet, *Le Jardin salutaire* (1483), to Charles VIII in order to be retained in his service. The boundary between the *escrivain*-scribe and the *escrivain*-author was porous, but their statuses were different.

CHAPTER TWO

The Question of the Author

A T THE OPENING OF HER *Lai du Chèvrefeuille*, Marie de France states that She is going to tell the truth about this lay, "Why it was composed, how and what are its origins" (Pur quei fu fez, coment e dunt). These are recognized as among the questions that make up what the Latin scholarly tradition calls the *accessus ad auctores*, a series of interrogations intended to facilitate the reading of the classics by explaining the life of the author, the title of the work, the intention of the writer, the subject of the book, the utility of its contents, and the branch of philosophy to which it belongs. These are Aristotelian categories and, to all authors who have gone through school, this grid is well known. In his *Light of the Laywomen* (*Lumière as Lais*), Pierre de Peckham (or de Fetcham) says it in this way: "Five things are now sought to be given at the beginning of the book: who was the author, and the title, and the matter and the form as well, and the goal, that is, for what reason the composition was made" (Cinq choses sont ja enquere/Au commencement en livere fere:/Ki fust autur, e l'entitlement,/E la matire e la furme ensement,/E le fin, ceo est par queu reisun/Fu fest la composiciun; ll. 531–536). This questionnaire allows us to measure literary awareness. Some use it as is, without making any modifications. The opening of the *Ars d'amour de vertu et de boneurté*, a treatise in prose from the end of the thirteenth century, reads: "For whom it was made and who made it, with these lines I shall describe it for you" (Pour qui est fait et ki le fist/Par ces vers ci le vous descrist). The riddle that comes next in the text has not been solved and we must keep in mind the contrast here between the affirmation of an author "who made it" and the desired or circumstantial anonymity that is emblematic of a very typical situation in medieval literature. Others parody, and even mock, this series of questions. For example, Jehan de Brie signs as "the good shepherd" (*le bon berger*) and writes *Le vray régime et gouvernement des Bergers et Bergères* (The True Regime and Government of the

Shepherds and Shepherdesses) for King Charles V. After having recalled the outline of the *accessus* and said that he would only answer part of them, he gives the title of his book: "And it will be called novelty"(Et sera appelé nouvelleté), a title that strictly speaking is not one. He adds, "And if one asks to what philosophical branch it belongs, one can respond that it will be attributed to foolosophy, or the philosophy of shepherding" (Et se aulcun demandoit à quelle partie de philosophie il sera supposé, on peult respondre que il sera attribué et supposé à la philosotie, ou philosophie de bergerie; p.6). The generality of the naming: "novelty" (*nouvelleté*) and the portemanteau word "foolosophy" contribute to the irony. The good shepherd is comically juxtaposing his function as shepherd and the scholarly pose he is taking, as one who is "worthy of reading [that is, to teach] in Fouarre street" (digne de lire en la rue au feurre)—the famous street of Parisian pupils whose name (*fouarre* = hay, straw) brings to mind sheep. Between the seriousness of the university and his parody, the function of the author must be deciphered.

Who Composes?

The allotment was not a purely social one, although there was, of course, a large divide between the religious orders and laymen. The religious orders, due to their way of life and their easy access to book culture, were more easily turned toward the production of books, especially in the earlier period. In reality, however, every layer of society, except the peasants, was found among those who composed works: monks and nuns, nobles and great lords, great and minor clerics, scholars, civil servants, members of the royal chancery,[1] of parlement, bourgeois, and merchants. The biggest separation, without a doubt, was between professionals and amateurs; those who made a living writing and those who composed solely for pleasure, to pass time in a useful way in later life. Knights, men of war, started writing at the point when one would have felt old in the Middle Ages: forty or fifty years of age. This is also what Antoine de La Sale [1385?–1461?] did.

The noble lord composing poetry is a well-attested figure in medieval literature. Guillaume IX, Richard the Lionheart, Conon de Béthune, Guy (Castellan of Couci), and Thibaut IV of Champagne were all very noble lords. Charles d'Orléans, René d'Anjou, and Thomas de Saluces, were noble princes of the fifteenth century. The configuration is also well in place in the imagination, since, as early as the thirteenth century, it was capable of arousing nostalgia. At its opening, the *Roman du Castelain de Couci et de la dame de Fayel* evokes the golden age when noble lords wrote: "But in olden days princes and counts made chants, stories, and games in rhymes of good manner" (Mais jadis li prince et li conte/Faisoient cans, dis et partures/En rimes de gente faitures; ll. 11–14). How did a noble lord learn to compose? We have the testimony of Conon de Béthune who learned from another noble lord, from his uncle Huon d'Oisy, who, he says, "taught me to sing when I was a child" (qui m'a apris a chanter des enfance). The lord, however, must not demean himself by becoming a remunerated poet. Peire d'Alvernhe makes this criticism via a series of satirical portraits of his peers. In the collection, he attacks two knights who had apparently become jongleurs: Grimoart Gausmar and Gonzalgo Roitz, whose true identities remain unknown.

The case of Philippe de Novare is of interest. The scion of a noble family from Novara in Italy, he lived in Cyprus, where he established ties with the lords of the Ibelin family. He presents himself as both a poet and as a man of war—he participated in the siege of the château de Deudamor in Cyprus where he was injured. The besieged rejoiced in his injury with the cry of "Your singer is dead, he has been killed!" (Mort est vostre chanteor, tué est!). But, according to his *Mémoires*, he had himself carried before the walls of the castle the next morning, where he sang a poem of defiance and mockery: "I am injured but I cannot keep quiet, in spite of it all, about master Renart and his company" (Nafré sui je, mais encore ne puis taire/De dan Renart et de sa compaignie; § LXVII). Philippe reports, indeed, on the quarrels between his lord and his adversary, Aimery Barlais, in the form of a "branch of Renart" (*branche de Renart*), in which he depicts himself with the traits of Chantecler, the rooster. What is more, Philippe is a great jurist: "the best litigant from here to the sea" (*le meilleur pledeour deça la mer*), Hugues de Brienne writes of him in 1263–1264. In short, Philippe de Novare was simultaneously a knight, a jurist, and a man of letters, combining the professions of arms and literature, as also did others, such as Jean de Joinville [1224?–1317], for example.

There is one case that seems most intriguing to contemporary eyes—that of authors who are completely ignorant of the scholarly culture. It is important to notice the astonishment shown by the anonymous author of the *Règles de la seconde rhétorique* in the fifteenth century in his list of authors worthy of serving as models for anyone who wishes to write poetry. He names Jean Brisebarre de Douay, who lived in "Machault's time," specifying, "and he was not a cleric and he did not know how to read or write in Latin" (et n'estoit point clers ne ne savoit lire n'escripre). In the opinion of this anonymous author, who was obviously a cleric himself, Brisebarre, in spite of everything, can be included in his gallery of famous authors: "for his texts were good" (car ses fais furent bons).

The Designation of a Function

A number of important terms designate the person who writes, reads, or recites poetry: jongleur, troubadour, trouvère, minstrel, cleric. Among the many functions of an entertainer, reciting epic poems or saints' lives and singing a troubadour's song belong to the jongleur. The minstrel, though, as is indicated in his name, has a ministry. He is attached to a court; to a lord whom he must entertain with stories or music. The further we advance in the Middle Ages, the more the terms for those who play instruments become specialized. Troubadours in the south and trouvères in the north mastered the art of *trobar*, of finding (*trouver*), of which the twelfth-century troubadour Jaufré Rudel says: "He who does not create melodies, does not know how to sing, as he who does not write verse knows not how to compose poetry" (No sap chantar qui so non di,/Ni vers trobar qui motz no fa). How did these different actors consider the profession that they practiced? In the prologue of *Erec and Enide*, Chrétien de Troyes, a cleric, protests against storytellers (*conteurs*), "Those who try to live by storytelling" (Cil qui de conter vivre vuelent; l. 22).

The question of the rapport, be it direct or indirect, with money, is essential in the distinction of status. Gautier de Coinci, a monk, who writes of the *Miracles of the Blessed Virgin*, does not want to be called a trouvère or a minstrel, if it is not, he says, of his Lady, the Virgin Mary. He defends the solemnity and the morality of his work. The jongleurs, condemned by the Church—with the exception of those who recite Lives of Saints—want to be recognized in all of their roles. A series of texts aims at showing that their service pleases God. For example, there is the beautiful tale of the *Tombeor Nostre Dame*, the jongleur of Our Lady who, not even knowing the *Ave Maria*, does somersaults in front of a statue of the Virgin to honor her. There is also the miracle *Du cierge qui descendi au jougleour* (the candle that came down to the jongleur) told by Gautier de Coinci, as well as the miracle of the Sainte-Chandelle d'Arras (the holy candle of Arras) that leads to the creation of a fraternity of jongleurs that is subsequently opened up to the bourgeois and the knights and is very active in Arras in the thirteenth century.

We know of the rivalries between jongleurs. At the beginning of the *Song of the Saxons*, Jean Bodel attacks "those bastard jongleurs" who do not know "the rich new lines, nor the rhymed song that Jean Bodel wrote" (Cil bastart jougleour . . . les riches vers nouviaus/Ne la chanson rimee que fist Jehans Bodiaux; ll. 31–32). Raimbert de Paris, in the prologue to the epic poem *Ogier de Danemark*, affirms his superiority: "There is no jongleur who is of his lineage" (Il n'est joglerres qui soit de son lignage; l. 186). In the *Supplication* that he addresses in 1274 to Alfonso X of Castile, Alfonso the Wise, Guiraut Riquier pleads for the establishment of a nomenclature for the diverse categories of people making a living from poetry. Following his advice, the king is said to have established four classes, four categories: jesters, jongleurs, troubadours and doctors of poetry, those who have the mastery *del sobiran trobar*, of the sovereign *trobar* (find).

Poetry is truly a *trade* in the medieval and modern sense of the term, a service and a job. A service, as in serving love or serving God, a job that one learns while working as a minstrel for a lord. Addressing his lord Henri III, duke of Brabant, Adenet le Roi recalls this at the end of *Cleomadés*: "And you taught me my trade" (Et me fist mon mestier apprendre; l. 18591). A trade: just as there are professionals of the materiality of writing, of copying, the *escrivains*, there are professionals of literary composition, a trade to which one must devote oneself. The formula that we find in Chrétien de Troyes, and elsewhere, is "put in his heart and all of his faculties" (*mettre son cuer et s'entente*). These same traits are referenced throughout the Middle Ages. Christine de Pizan, in the dedication of a manuscript of her complete works to Isabeau of Bavaria, speaks of her "labor and long work" (*labour et lonc travail*; l. 73) and of "her effort" (*son entencion*). Then again, authors are proud of pointing out that this work is not a manual trade. Rutebeuf repeats it time and again in his work: "I am not a manual laborer" (ne sui ovriers de mains; *Mariage Rutebeuf*, l. 98). Jean Froissart, a priest, takes up the theme in *Le Joli Buisson de Jonece*: "You neither labor nor work at any manual effort" (Tu ne labeures ne travelles/De nulle painne manuele; ll. 170–171). This trade by itself, which is not that of a "manual laborer" (*manouvrier*), to use Froissart's term (l. 184), is described in a laudative manner. For Watriquet de Couvin in the *Dit du fol menestrel*, it is the *biau mestier* (beautiful trade); for Jean Froissart, who recounts words spoken by Gaston Phebus in the *Dit du Florin*: "It is a beautiful occupation, my friend, to make such things" (C'est uns beaus mestiers,/Beaus maistres de faire telz choses; ll. 298–299), likewise *le beau mestier*. When referring specifically to his writings on love, Froissart speaks of "joyful trade" (*gai mestier*) in *La Prison amoureuse* (l. 288) or of "noble trade" (*mestier gens*) in *Le Joli Buisson de Jonece* (l. 162).

This occupation differentiates the person who gives himself to the craft from the amateur and becomes a topos of modesty for those who present themselves as not being professionals: "Beginning gives me great cause for worry as I am not instructed in this trade" (Mes molt me dout au commencier,/car duiz ne sui de tel mestier; ll. 322–323), admits the author of the *Roman de la Poire*. One gets the feeling that, in the medieval mind-set, practiced with devotion, writing will raise a person up above his/her condition. With the passing of the centuries, we see it become a mission. A new type of French writer then appears, whom we may dare to call a *poet*, like the great writers of Antiquity. It is the figure of Guillaume de Machaut and the image he presents of himself in the prologue that crowns his complete works: he is worthy of receiving gifts from Nature and from Love. This image is confirmed by his disciple Eustache Deschamps, who refers to him with the enthusiastic terms: "Noble poet and renowned versifier," "noble rhetoric," "worldly god of harmony"(*Noble poete et faiseur renommé*, ballad 447, vol. 3; *noble rethorique*; ballad 123, tome I; *mondain dieu d'armonie*; ballad 124).

Boccaccio defines the status of poet in a chapter of his *De Casibus virorum illustrium* (3.16). Here, the position of poet fits in a series that recalls the three orders of society: the knight, the legist (this is Boccaccio's version of the cleric), and the laborer. In a way, he creates a fourth state—that of the poet—which he works at characterizing in relation to the other three. At the beginning of the fifteenth century, Laurent de Premierfait translated the passage as follows: "the poet searches for and inhabits solitary places" (le poète quier et habite lieux solitaires); "the knight rejoices in weapons and noise" (le chevalier s'esjouist en armes et en bruit); "the legist rejoices in disputes and argumentation" (le legiste s'esjouist en riotes et en plaiz); and "the laborer rejoices in beauty and in the fertility of fields" (le laboureur s'esjouist en beauté et en planteur-euseté de champs).

In distinguishing the poet, Boccaccio develops three other associations: "the poet rejoices in listening to the melody of his simple songs" (le poete s'esjouist ou son de ses chansonnettes), "the poet enjoys himself in con-templation" (le poete se soulace en contemplacion), "the poet believes that fame can give happiness" (le poete cuide que renommee puisse don-ner bieneurté). This reflection on the poet becomes an important part of theoretical thought about literature in the fifteenth century. Poets deal with the fable—let us remember that Plato had them expelled from the city. Clerics, however, deal with knowledge. In the *Champion des Dames*, Martin le Franc, a renowned and vicious adversary of women, places two categories in opposition: "Poets have nothing but gossip in their mouths and according to their desires they tell their lying tales. Clerics must not mention their nonsense" (Poetes n'ont que baverie/Et a leur gré font fiction./On ne doibt de leur jenglerie/Entre clercs faire mention; ll. 15085–15088).

The Author's Self-Awareness

Authors name themselves, either in the first or third person, and generally also state their places of birth or origin: "My name is Marie and I come from France" (Marie ai nun, si sui de France); introduce the title of the work, "Chrétien begins his book about the Knight of the Cart" (Del Che-valier de la Charrete/Comance Crestïens son livre); or mention previous works, almost as in an advertisement. A series of authors from the twelfth to the fifteenth centuries employ such techniques, including Chrétien de Troyes in *Cligés*, Jean Bodel in the fabliau of the *Deus chevaus*, Adenet le Roi in *Cleomadés*, Jean Froissart in *Le Joli Buisson de Jonece*. The formula introducing the list of works is most often "the one who wrote" (Cil qui fit) or "I who wrote" (je qui fis), or "the one who found" (cil qui trouva).

We also find authors who quote themselves either openly or in a concealed manner within their work. Gautier d'Arras concludes his second romance, *Ille et Galeron*, by referring to his first, *Eracle*. Philippe de Novare finishes his *Quatre tenz d'aage d'ome* by enumerating and analyzing the entirety of his production: "Philippe de Novare, who wrote this book, wrote two others" (*Phelipes de Novare, qui fist cest livre, en fist autres .II.*). Christine de Pizan systematically practices this promotion of her work.

But the presence of an author's name is at times subject to manipulation by scribes. There are numerous lyrical pieces in the collections that we call songbooks (*chansonniers*) that are attributed or reattributed in various ways by the copyists. There are various reasons for this: ignorance, inadvertence, but also specific literary sentiments. In the songbooks of the troubadours, we see pieces going from the name of one poet to that of another, because their style seems to be more like that of one or the other. This game takes place, for example, between the *cansos* by Guillaume IX and Jaufré Rudel. Along the same lines, the celebrity of the latter's "Lanquan li jorn son lon en may" (When the days are long in May) leads some manuscripts to attribute all of the poems beginning with "Lanquan . . . " to him. This phenomenon can also be seen elsewhere. In his *Regret Nostre Dame*, Huon le Roi de Cambrai names himself twice: as "Li Rois de Cambrai" in the first stanza and as "Hues li Rois" (Hues is the subject form of Huon) in stanza 234. An inattentive scribe, influenced no doubt by the name of an epic hero, replaced the line "Li Rois de Cambrai" in the first stanza with the name of the hero of the chanson de geste *Raoul de Cambrai*. In the thirteenth-century *Livre de Philosophie et de Moralité* by Alart de Cambrai, the author names himself: "I, Alart who am from Cambrai" (Je, Alars qui sui de Cambrai). Two of the nine manuscripts that conserve this text, however, give different names: "I, Andreis who am from Huy" (Je, Andreis qi fu nez de Huy), and "I, Jehan, who have had little instruction" (Jou Jehans qi pois ai de letre). What does this instability tell us? That the name appears in the text because the author wanted it there, but that it was malleable in the eyes of the scribes. For them, there is an authorial function that is more important than individual authors, and it can be reattributed.

The author can also become a character. Raoul de Houdenc names himself at the end of the *Songe d'Enfer* as narrator and author: "Raoul takes leave, here he awakes" (Congié prent Raouls, si s'esveille; l. 672), "Raoul de Houdenc, without lying/ . . . made this fable from his dream" (Raouls de Houdaing, sans mençonge/ . . . cest fablel fist de son songe; ll. 677–678), but he is also a character inside the story. The allegories speak to him using his name: "Raoul, you are welcome" (Raoul, bien soies-tu venuz; l. 412), say Pilate and Belzébuth.

Guillaume de Machaut plays a similar game in the *Jugement du Roi de Navarre*. While taking a walk, the poet is seen by a lady, who will turn out to be an allegory: Boneürté [Happiness]. She inquires of her squire about the identity of the character she has met, who was absorbed in thought: "That is Guillaume de Machaut" (C'est la Guillaumes de Machaut; l. 573), replies the squire. At this point in the text, Guillaume de Machaut is a character. He is the author when he signs his text: "I, Guillaume named above, who am surnamed from Machaut" (Je, Guillaumes dessus nommez,/Qui de Machau sui seurnommez; ll. 4199–4200). The name reunites the two faces of the writer and his creature.

The narrator inside the story is often designated by the name of *acteur*. This is the case, for example, in *Le Débat du Vieil et du Jeune* (The Debate of the Old Man and the Young) by Blosseville, a fifteenth-century poet of the Blois court. In this text, he assumes the position of an "embedded" narrator who is going to serve as secretary to the debaters. The latter call him by his authorial name: "For they called me Blosseville and gently asked me if I had heard the debate" (Car Blosseville me nommerent,/Et doulcement me demanderent/Se le debat avoye ouy; ll. 364–366).

The book can identify its author too, in a sort of metapersonification. Simon de Freine signs his two major works, *Le Roman de Philosophie* and *La Vie de saint Georges*, in acrostics with the formula: "Simon de Freine wrote me" (Simund de Freine me fist), as if the book were speaking. This intrication of postures reveals the richness and complexity of the literary creation.

To Sign One's Work

In the Middle Ages, a person's name was his Christian name, which for us is the first name. Fustel de Coulanges notes this in *La Cité antique*: Christianity introduced a revolution in naming compared with the standard practices of the Roman world. What completes the medieval Jeans, Guillaumes, Raouls is an indication of origin—de Meun, de Machaut —, a title, or a nickname. To sign a work and to have one's name figure within the work is less of a revelation of identity than it is the construction of a parchment character, the imposition of a figure, giving it a label. The Latin poetry of the Goliards, for example, is filled with collective names—Golias, Primas, Gautier—that refer to a mythical or emblematic figure. Just as the knights can have telling coats of arms on their shields, texts contain telling names, *senhals* (code names), or signs. The name gives meaning, often functioning like a metaphor. The reader, medieval or modern, must know how to draw out this meaning, how to "interpret" the name. He must also know how to "extract the sense" (*le sens estraire*) from the names, says the Recluse of Molliens in the *Romance of Charity* (stanza 95), who goes about it feverishly. This goes for proper names as well as for common nouns. Many medieval authors believed in the tie between names and things, whether it be an echo of Plato's theories on the motivation of names—Cratylism—or that the Middle Ages gave full weight to the passage in Genesis where God names and, in naming, creates. "Nomina sunt cunsequentia rerum"—names are consequential to things. This dictum is found throughout the entire period in jurists' writings. The formula is in Dante's *Vita nova* (13.4). It is translated by Chrétien de Troyes in the teachings of Perceval's mother: "By the name, we know the man" (Par lo sornon conoist en l'ome; l. 526).

But before speaking about names, we first have to find them. Why do medieval authors hide their names? There are reasons of a moral nature, humility with regards to the world—"to avoid vainglory" (pour vaine gloire eschiver)—or with regards to the matter—too high, too holy. This is the case with works by certain monastic authors, such as the author of the *Chastel Perilleux* who has his book say: "Let the author's name be sealed" (Le nom de l'acteur soit cellés; Prologue of BNF, fr. 1882). The reason for such secrecy can be of a social nature. Jean de le Mote, the author of the *Parfait du Paon*, declares: "Were I not from poverty, inside I would name myself" (Se povretés n'estoit, dedens me nemeroie; l. 3891), which he does anyway in the following stanza, the last one of his text, but by means of an acrostic. The Middle Ages appreciated these hidden signatures, and the acrostics and anagrams are numerous.

At other times, the name can be affirmed with pride. This is particularly the case with poets who depend on a patron. Jean de Condé affirms in the *Dit des Jacobins et des Fremeneurs*: "If you wish to know my name, I am Jean de Condé and am famous in many places" (Se savoir volés mon droit non, / Jehans de Condé sui nommés, / Qui sui en mains lieus renommés; ll. 312–314).

The name is at times highlighted according to a solemn and significant construction. Dante exemplifies this in the *Divine Comedy* when, after refusing to give his name in canto 14 of the *Purgatory*, has it pronounced by Beatrice in canto 30, at the moment when she takes Virgil's place. In a way, the name Dante, "he who gives," according to the etymology proposed by Boccaccio, is *given* to him by the beloved woman. Here Dante reproduces a pattern from the Romanesque literature of the twelfth century. In Chrétien de Troyes' works, Lancelot is referred to only by the paraphrase that, in its paradox, defines him, "the Knight of the Cart," until Queen Guinevere, well into the romance, pronounces his name. It is only after two-thirds of Proust's *Recherche*, as Jacqueline Risset notes, that the first name Marcel resonates. Again in Chrétien de Troyes, it is only after the scene of the Grail that Perceval "guesses" his name:

> Et cil qui son non ne savoit
> Devine et dit que il avoit
> Percevaus li Gualois a non,
> Ne ne set s'il dit voir o non   (ll. 3511–3514)

(And the youth, who did not know his name, guessed and said he was called Perceval the Welshman. But although he did not know if that were true or not; ed. Kibler, p. 425)

The name is a revelation.

Nomen-omen, name omen, name fate, the name is a program of life. One must inhabit one's name. Rutebeuf, "who works very hard" (qui rudement euvre), Rutebeuf, "who is said to be of coarseness and of beef" (qui est dit de rude et de boeuf), delivers with his name a status, a function and a poetic. This poetic implies work—it is in this that it is a "coarse" (*rude*) poetic—that does not rely on inspiration. However, Rutebeuf clarifies, it is a work that is not manual: "I am not a manual laborer" (Je ne suis pas ouvrier de mains), the paradoxical labor of a lazy person, "who does not willingly rise early" (Qui ne lief pas volentiers main). Rute-beuf creates a goliard character of himself, amateur of wine and of dice. Eustache Deschamps draws out all of the possibilities of his different names: Eustache Deschamps, Eustache Morel, building a persona around a network of images induced by these names, between the Moor, by his color, and morality by his name and his place of birth, Vertus (virtue). Jean Gerson plays with languages recalling that his Christian name, Jean, signifies "grace" in Hebrew. In the same way his cognomen, "Gerson," taken from the village where he was born, designates in the same language the foreigner or the pilgrim. Jean Le Fèvre works the image evoked by his nickname, that of the smith (le fèvre); Jean Molinet, thanks to the image of a mill (moulin), creates a picturesque signature of himself that he imposes on his works: the mill that transforms a raw material, the grain, into a fine flour becomes the symbol of his writing. We are taken from the signature to the portrait of a condition and to poetic art.

Portrait of a Condition

When they do so, authors generally refer to themselves, insofar as they are poets, with a distinctive, coded mark, like a birthmark. Most often this mark is ugliness; modeled upon the legendary ugliness of Socrates, of Aesop, or of Aristotle. Whether the chosen trait is real or fictional, it is to be taken for something other than its face value. It draws a portrait of humility, even humiliation of the cleric in comparison with the knight, or of the poor cleric in comparison with the rich layman. Nicknamed the Hunchback (le Bossu) in Arras, Adam de la Halle protests in his Chanson du roi de Sicile: "They call me hunchback, but I am not that at all" (On m'apele Bochu, mais je ne le sui mie; laisse 4, l. 70), implying that this nickname is hereditary. This does not stop his principal rival in his jeux-partis, Jean Bretel, a rich bourgeois, prince Du Puy, from playing with this nickname to disqualify Adam's arguments in a humorous way: "And he responds to me too much like a hunchback" (Et trop me respondés bochuement; Jeu-parti 11, l. 88). The qualification is both criticism and homage.

Just as in logic, there are arguments that are horned (cornus) and sophisms that are hunchbacked (bossus)—one character from the fabliau La Contregengle reproaches the other "You speak to me in too crazy of a manner and you give me an argument and a sophism that are totally hunchbacked" (Tu paroles moult folement./Si me fez si .I. argument/Et .I. sofisme tout boçu)—there is likewise a "hunchbacked" way of reasoning about love. But to name a style with another proper name is also to recognize a talent attached or intrinsic to Adam.

The two authors of *Congés*, Jean Bodel and Baude Fastoul, are without a doubt lepers, but they use their disease like a brand that distinguishes and "alienates" (*estrange*) them. Guillaume de Machaut calls himself one-eyed. Jean de Meun, nicknamed Jean Clopinel, *clopiner* meaning to limp, represents himself as lame just as Jean Le Fèvre uses his name, the smith, and the physical attribute of being lame to present himself as a Vulcan. Philippe de Mézières implies that he stutters; Eustache Deschamps plays on his bald spot. Guillaume de Machaut, Eustache Deschamps, and Jean Molinet all imply that they are sexually impotent. In a suggestive manner, the metaphor through which Molinet reveals this shortcoming is of a scriptural nature: "I have no more ink in my inkwell" (Je n'ai plus d'encre en mon cornet), just as Jean Bodel refers to the white traces that leprosy leaves on the skin with the verb *rimer*—"cover with frost," "chap or crack"—which is homonymous with the literary act *rimer* (to rhyme or put into verse): "I flourish in winter and when it is summer I rhyme/cover with frost" (Que je floris quant il yverne/Et quant il fait esté je rime; ll. 197–198).

All of these traits, indeed, turn back into marks of the chosen or elite. Hunchbacked? Doesn't Virgil pass as a hunchback in the Middle Ages? The author of *Renart le Contrefait*, in the fourteenth century, describes the poet in these words: "Virgil was subtle and wise in the use of laws and arts. He was short in stature and a little hunchbacked by nature" (Soubtil fu Virgille et sage/De loix et des ars et d'uzage./Il fu de petite estature; Bochu fu un pou par nature; ll. 34303–34306). Bald? Wasn't Saint Paul "without hair in front" (*pelé devant*)? Stutterer? Moses stuttered and, at any rate, God made Balaam's ass speak and makes whomever He wishes eloquent.

The portrait is situated somewhere between derision, stigmatization and glorification. Derision: this is the portrait that François Villon gives of himself, "An old monkey is always unpleasant" (Toujours viel singe est desplaisant). Glorification: the biblical passage of when Jacob meets the angel is present in the minds of the clerics. *Le Mistère du Viel Testa-*

ment (The Mystery of the Old Testament) evokes it. As a sign of his being chosen, Jacob changes his name after this encounter: he becomes Israel and starts to *clocher*, to limp.

The Fictions of the Author

The name gives permission. Great works in prose from the thirteenth century are placed under the authority of a fictitious author's name. The act that inscribes the work in comparison with those that precede it indicates this power of the name. The name can be usurped; it can be invented in a significant onomastic game. Usurped, like the name of Walter Map that figures at the end of the *Quest del Saint Graal* (Quest of the Holy Grail) and at the beginning of the *Mort le Roi Artu* (Death of King Arthur). The historical Walter Map, born around 1135, wrote in Latin for Henry II Plantagenet, in particular his *De nugis curialium* (Of the Frivolities of the Courtiers). Helie de Boron, in the epilogue of the *Prose Tristan*, attributes the *Lancelot* to him. But Helie de Boron is, itself, an invented name that combines a biblical name, "Helie," with a fragment of the name Robert de Boron, who authored a section of *Merlin,* as well as an *Estoire dou Graal* or *Joseph d'Arimathie* (Story of the Grail) in verse. Robert de Boron is then credited with the prose trilogy composed of the *Joseph*, the *Merlin*, and the *Perceval.* The name functions as a guarantor.

Fictitious as well, the author who presents himself at the beginning of the *Prose Tristan* saying, "I, Luce, knight and lord, of the Castle del Gat" (Je, Luces, chevaliers et sires, del Chastel del Gat), gives information about himself in the quite typical form of the personal charters that aim at authenticating the story that will follow. He is a knight and, therefore, a part of the world of heroes that he is going to evoke. He is "a close neighbor of Salisbury" (*voisin prochien de Salesbieres*). And it is in the library of Salisbury, according to the *Queste*, that "Master Walter Map" found the adventures told by Bors and from which he made "his book of the Holy Grail" (*son livre del Saint Graal*). Fiction feeds the fiction that must guarantee the truth.

There is within these texts, in fact, a portrait of the ideal author; Merlin, son of the devil and a virgin. He knows of things past thanks to his diabolical ancestry and of things to come thanks to God. He dictates his book to a scribe, Blaise, and this duo functions according to the model of the prophetic word and the written text. We find an analogous game in the field of the epic poem and the chronicle: Turpin, the archbishop in the *Song of Roland*, receives a chronicle in Latin, the *Historia Karoli Magni et Rotholandi*, known as the *Pseudo-Turpin Chronicle*, that dates back to the middle of the twelfth century and that has known a huge success.

The models for songs, however, are of a diverse nature, borrowing from different registers that feed the medieval imagination. In the natural world, the model is the bird, specifically the nightingale. The direct comparison of the poet with the bird is frequent. Beginning with the troubadours. Just as the nightingale (*rossignol*) "modulates his sweet song" (refranh son dous chantar), says Jaufre Rudel, in *Lo rius de la fontana*, "it is only appropriate that I modulate mine" (Dreitz es qu'ieu lo mieu refranha). Implicitly, the comparison is noted by the naming of jongleurs: "Friend Nightingale" (*Ami Rossignol*), found in Raimbaut of Orange; by the naming of minstrels that appear as characters in narrative texts: "Sparrow" (*Pinchonnet*) in *Cleomadés*; by the metaphorical designation of poets themselves. Guillaume Crétin signs the quatrain that he addresses to Brother Jean Martin with this formula: "the G [pronounced jay] of the woods, alias Cretin" (le G. du bois, alias Cretin). The expression can be read in two ways. The letter gives the initial of the first name: Guillaume, but also, when it is pronounced: the bird, the jay. *Du bois* (of the woods) gives the name, perhaps, but also the place of residence of the bird poet, the woods of Vincennes.

The image of the poet as a bird, a major figure in songs, can incarnate other values for him as well: freedom, in particular, of which the court poet dreams. This is the use that Eustache Deschamps makes of it. He compares the bird *engeolé*—put in a cage, a prison, a *geole*—and that no longer sings, to the bird of the fields (Deschamps) that flies and sings. The bird can designate the various functions of poetry: love with the nightingale, the freedom of the satyr, for Eustache Deschamps; the praise of God, for Guillaume de Digulleville who uses the image of the lark (*alouette*), in which he finds a pseudo-etymology linking it to *lauda*, praise. The other figures of the poet can be borrowed from the world of mythology, this would be Orpheus; or from the Bible, with David.

Interest in the Author in the Middle Ages

Some great figures from Antiquity are seen as authorities, guarantors. In the domain of philosophy, first and foremost there is Aristotle; "the" philosopher for the Middle Ages. For literature, the two names that come up the most often are Virgil and Ovid. Their lives are studied. Their works are commented on—most often in Latin—cited and even dreamt about. These great authors become characters in the medieval imaginary world. Thus, Aristotle is a hero in the *Lai d'Aristote*, whose attribution to Henry d'Andeli is debated today. The text is now attributed to Henry de Valenciennes. Aristotle's misadventure: accepting, out of loving desire, to be changed into a beast of burden and ridden by a scheming woman is a popular exemplum that leads to numerous iconographic representations. Another familiar topic is the instruction he is said to have given to Alexander. Rutebeuf writes a *Dit d'Aristote*, a short text containing advice to a prince that he takes from Walter of Châtillon's *Alexandreis*. Richard de Fournival names Ovid as the author and hero of *De Vetula* (On the Old Woman), translated into French in the fourteenth century by Jean Le Fèvre. Virgil appears in numerous works in the role of a magician. He teaches astrology to the emperor's son in the *Dolopathos* and magic to a fairy in the *Roman d'Escanor* by Girart d'Amiens—the syncretism is notable. Some medieval authors rise to this level of notoriety. Such is the case of Jean de Meun, who functions as a character in Honoré Bovet's *Apparition Maître Jean de Meun* or in the *Pèlerinage maistre Jean de Meun*, incunable of 1484. The name Jean de Meun acts then as a "seat of coherence," to use Michel Foucault's words, making possible the texts of these later authors.

This interest in the author stands out as well in the phenomenon of the *vidas* and the *razos* for the troubadours. These are lives extrapolated from works that precede the sections of songbooks dedicated to these authors and from the commentaries that are provided with the songs. This practice demonstrates a profound interest in a literature that works texts like a matter for dreams and writing. The same movement gives birth to a romance: *Le Roman du Castelain de Couci et de la Dame de Fayel*, whose hero, Renaut, has for role model Guy, the castellan of Coucy-le-Château. The romance, which makes use of the theme of the eaten heart, inserts poems by the trouvère that he puts in the mouth of his character. The

Roman de Joufroi de Poitiers takes as the matrix for its hero, so it seems, the troubadour Guillaume IX, count of Poitiers and duke of Aquitaine. He brings in a minstrel character named Marchabrun, an allusion to the troubadour Marcabru. Some authors do the work of a *razo* on their own production. This is one way to look at Dante's *Vita nova* and Guillaume de Machaut's *Voir-dit*. Finally, Villon, by playing with the juridical form of a will, subverts the notion of authority all the while feigning to reinforce it. He ends up by building a fiction of himself that has long fed the critical dreams of his readers.

Some authors, whom we can identify from the deference shown to them by posterity and the frequency of the citing of their names, define moments in medieval literature: Chrétien de Troyes in the twelfth century, after whom a few of his successors found it difficult to write. This is affirmed by Huon de Méry, with the help of the metaphor of gleaning, in his *Tournoiemenz Antecrit*. He praises Chrétien's "beautiful French" (*bel françois*). The anonymous author of the romance *Hunbaut* praises his "good poems" (*bons dis*); Sarrasin in the *Roman du Hem* cites the "very beautiful romance that Chrétien made of Perceval" (remant que Crestiens/Trova si bel de Perceval). In the thirteenth century, Jean de Meun has a similar status. The *Romance of the Rose*, and the formula "where the art of love is all enclosed" (où l'art d'amour est tout enclose) is a challenge and a trigger for many works.[2] And this goes on until the sixteenth century and probably further. A *Coq a l'asne*, conserved in a manuscript of the National Library of Vienna, 10203, questions, with irony:

> Pourquoy lisons nous l'evangille,
> Puisque le pape en est marry?
> Il vauldroit mieulx, par sainct Marry,
> Lire le rommand de la Rose,
> Ou l'on voit toute amour enclose
> Ou bien les espitres d'Ovide.   (ll. 186–191)

(Why do we read the Gospel since the pope is angered by it? It would be better, by Holy Mary, to read the Romance of the Rose, where we find all of love enclosed, or perhaps Ovid's epistles).

Alain Chartier, at the beginning of the fifteenth century, and Georges Chastellain, at the end, are seen as markers of moments in literature. As early as the sixteenth century, Alain Chartier is qualified as "the father of French eloquence" both by Pierre Fabri in his *Great and True Art of Rhetoric*, a text whose royal privilege is dated 1520, and by Jean Bouchet in his *Annales d'Aquitaine* of 1524; Georges Chastellain is distinguished by the formula "the great Georges." Literary history, with its characteristic love for labeling adjectives, and its allocation of glory, is in place.

CHAPTER THREE

The Work and Its Audiences

THE "AUTHOR," WHETHER REAL OR FICTITIOUS, who guarantees the text with the formula "the tale says that . . . ," certainly held a role in the medieval mental toolbox. However, the relationship of the author's name to history is not unequivocal. It plays on different levels and according to various modes of significance. Another function plays an essential role in the emergence of the literary work: the intended recipient.

The Command to Write

Indeed, upon whom or what does the decision to write depend? The author can claim to be responding to a personal desire. The formula is then, "The fancy strikes me to . . . " (talent m'est pris de . . .). A category of authors who are not dependent stands out: nobles and religious, for whom writing, or singing, is not a material necessity: "I will fashion a song, for the fancy strikes me" (Chançon ferai, que talenz m'en est pris), says Theobald of Champagne. "The desire has come to me to remember a lay that I heard tell of" (Talenz me prist de remembrer/un lai dont j'ai oï parler), notes Marie de France at the opening of the *Lai du Chaitivel*. "I feel the desire to continue telling you" (Talens me prent qu'ancor vos cont), affirms Gautier de Coincy in the second part of his collection of *Miracles*. And if a dependent author gives in to such a dream, it is in the form of a wish: "May I begin to tell that which my heart dictates to me!" (Puissé je commancier a dire/Ce que mes cuers m'a endité!), ventures Rutebeuf at the opening of the *Ordres de Paris*. Philippe Mousket finds it useful to specify that he translated his *Chronicle*, from the Latin of the Chronicle of the abbey of Saint-Denis into *roumans* (French), "without request and without command" (sans proiïères et sans coumans; l. 12). In point of fact, the most common situation is that of the order, which can come in two different forms: the plea, when the request comes from a friend or a peer, and the command, when the request emanates from a superior. These nuances are perceived and analyzed perfectly. At the end of the fifteenth century, in the prologue of his *Condamnation de Banquet*, Nicolas de la Chesnaye specifies:

> The author or composer of such works can oftentimes be so strongly called upon and beseeched by his superiors or by a proven friend, or by others from whom requests are seen as orders, that he is forced (in obeying) to put hand and quill to such an elegant or foreign matter that it transcends the summit of his intelligence.

> (L'acteur ou compositeur de telles oeuvres peut souventesfois estre si fort requi et sollicité par plus grans de soy ou par aucuns esprouvez amys, ou par autres desquelz les requestes luy tiennent lieu de commandement, qu'il est contraint (en obeyssant) mettre la main et la plume a matiere si elegante ou peregrine que elle transcede la summité de son intelligence.)

In the thirteenth century, the author of the romance *Richard le Beau*, calls himself "Mestre Requis" (Master Requested; l. 73).

The possibility of an unconditional command exists, when the order comes from God. Such is the case of the writings of the mystics. In the *Scivias*, Hildegard von Bingen speaks of this order: "Say and write what you see and hear" (Dis et écris ce que tu vois et entends). The patron is generally a lord or lady. Marie of Champagne, for instance, for Chrétien de Troyes in the *Knight of the Cart*: "Since my lady of Champagne wishes me to begin a romance" (Puis que ma dame de Champaigne/Vialt que romans a feire anpraigne). There is also Philip of Alsace in the *Conte du Graal* and Guy de Chatillon at the opening of the *Chroniques* by Jean Froissart: "At the request and for the contemplation and pleasure of my lord Guy de Chatillon" (A la requeste, contemplation et plaisance de messire Guy de Chastillon).

Froissart uses the identical formula for the two manuscripts that comprise his *dittiés* (compositions) and love treatises written "at the request and for the contemplation and pleasure of several high and noble lords and of several noble and brave ladies" (a la requeste et contemplation et plaisance de pluisours haus et nobles signours et de pluisours nobles et vaillans dames). The order can come from a beloved lady who appears in the figure of suzerain: "My lady orders and prays me to tell her of an adventure that happened to the Good Knight [that is, Gawain]" (Ma dame me commande et prie/Que une aventure li die/Qu'il avint au Bon Chevalier), the [anonymous thirteenth-century Arthurian romance] *L'Âtre Périlleux* (The Perilous Graveyard) begins.

Another configuration puts forward a more abstract power, an allegory, generally Love. In lyrical poetry the accepted expression is "Love orders me to sing " (Amour me semont de chanter). Alternating in these opening lines of texts, therefore, are an affirmed desire: "Desire has struck me to sing" (Talent m'est pris de chanter) and a hidden desire masked by an abstraction, by a power that controls the will of the poet: Love. The formula can be broken down when the poet enumerates the components necessary for being in a suitable situation for love: "The new season, the month of May, the violet and the nightingale order me to sing" (Li nouviaux tanz et mais et violete/Et lousseignolz me semont de chanter; Chastelain de Coucy). A similar presentation exists for allegorical texts, such as the *Romance of the Rose* in the thirteenth century: "Now I wish to rhyme this dream/ . . . /that Love asks and orders of me" (Or veil cel songe rimeer/ . . . /qu'Amors le me prie et commande; ll. 32 and 34), and for Jean Froissart's *Orloge amoureux* in the fourteenth century: "Love . . . orders and summons me to write of my state" (Amours/[...] m'ordonne/Et me semont de mon estat trettier; ll. 37–39).

As the centuries go by, we observe in these formulae a shift from song to writing, from singing about to writing about. The function of the poet, then, ends up being modified. By Love's order, he becomes the secretary of his own heart. He notes, he transcribes.

The most beautiful formulation is perhaps that of Dante. In Canto 24 of *Purgatory*, we read: "I am one who, when Love inspires me, note" (I' mi son un che, quando/Amor mi spira, noto; ll. 52–53). Love whispers, inspires, the poet notes. Another change takes place: Love is no longer the only power giving the order to write. Christine de Pizan, in *Le Livre de la Mutacion de Fortune*, praises the nobles saying: "but the noble voice [that is, fame] orders me to write of their ways. That which must not be silenced but said" (mais la noble voix/De leurs meurs me semont d'escripre/Ce qu'on ne doit taire, mais dire; ll. 5434–5436). In Alain Chartier's *Livre des quatre Dames*, the fourth lady, whose beloved ran from the field of battle at Agincourt, proclaims: "The strength of the pain forces me to expose my very shameful case that makes me break down in tears" (Force de dueil me vient cemondre/De mon cas treshonteux expondre,/Qui me fait toute en lermes fondre; ll. 2552–2554). The song is born from joy or procures joy; the written text at the end of the Middle Ages can be said to be born from sadness.

From the Command to the Dedication

The command can be formulated indirectly. Thus we see the author offer his book in an often-formal dedication in hopes of gaining a material or symbolic profit: "to acquire honor and prize" (pour acquérir honneur et prix). Marie de France does this in the second part of her prologue to the *Lais*, where she is addressing King Henry II Plantagenet: "In your honor, noble king, you who are so valiant and courtly, . . . I have undertaken to gather these lays" (En l'onur de vus, nobles reis,/ki tant estes pruz et curteis/ . . . /m'entremis des lais assembler; ll. 43–44 and 47).

Gautier d'Arras begins *Eracle* for the brother of Comte Henri I, *dit le Libéral*, of Champagne, Thibaut de Blois, whom he eulogizes, saying: "for him I have undertaken this work" (por lui ai jou ceste oevre emprise; l. 86). Later in the romance, he adds, "I did it thanks to him, I do not seek to deny it, and thanks also to the countess [Henri's wife, Marie de Champagne]" (Par lui le fis, nel quier noïer,/et par le contesse autressi; ll. 6526–6527). It is important to note the nuance between the *por* (for), indicating the intention in the beginning and the *par* (thanks to), signaling the means obtained in order to achieve this intended result. In the end, Gautier offers the work to Baldwin of Hainaut, an ally of the Blois-Champagne family: "Count Baldwin, I give it to you" (Quens Bauduin, a vos l'otroi; l. 6559), but with the warning that he will "place" the book elsewhere if he is not adequately compensated.

In one way or another, authors must address the question of remuneration, and the choice of a generous patron is a matter of strategy. This financial dependency leads to the posture of beggar and the technique of the multiple offer. Wace congratulates himself at the beginning of the third part of his *Roman de Rou* for having obtained a prebend in Bayeux thanks to Henry II [of England], but he is nostalgic for the generosity of yesteryear when the nobles paid to have their name "in a historical text" (*en estoire*; l. 149). Now, he says, it is hard to find somebody who will give enough money to pay a scribe for one month (ll. 154–156). At the end of the *Rou*, after the king has withdrawn his commission to give it to Benoît de Sainte-Maure, Wace reminds Benoît that the king did not keep all of his promises: "He gave me much, he promised me even more" (Mult me duna, plus me pramist; l. 11426).

What are these authors, who moreover are not all jongleurs, asking for? Money, position, a coat, a horse. "Lord 'Truchement,' if only I had a good horse" (Drogoman sénher, s'eu agués bon destrier), says Peire Vidal. Guillaume de Machaut and Eustache Deschamps also ask for a horse. Indeed, all could sing along with Guillaume de Machaut: "Give, lords, give generously" (Donnez, signeurs, donnez à toutes mains).

In order to obtain these gifts, and increasingly more when the book reaches a specific market value, authors tend to have several copies of their manuscripts made: copies that they then dedicate to different lords. Christine de Pizan demonstrates this. She writes the *Livre des fais et Bonnes meurs du Sage roy Charles V* to satisfy an order from the duke of Burgundy, Philip the Bold, brother of the king. But her patron dies while she is still writing. She deplores his death in the beginning of part 2. She offers the finished work to the duke of Berry as a New Year's gift on January 1, 1405, and another copy to the son of her patron, John the Fearless who, on February 20, 1406, has one hundred crowns given to Christine for this book and another.

A contemporary of Christine's, Honoré Bovet, does the same thing for his *Apparition Maistre Jean de Meun*. He presents copies with dedications to Louis, duke of Orleans; to the duke of Burgundy; to Valentine Visconti, duchess of Orleans; and, lastly, as understood from the coat of arms represented in the first miniature of the manuscript dedicated to him, to Jean de Montaigu, favorite of Charles VI. He specifies to him that it is the copy of the one that he sent to the duke of Orleans and that he is sending him "on this blessed day a New Year's gift" (a cestuy benoyst jour des estreines).

Prologues and Epilogues

The way to begin a text is codified by rhetoric. Following Cicero's example, Brunetto Latini, in his *Livre du Tresor*, analyzes the different types of prologues according to the desired effect and the matters being introduced, for there are rules to follow for the prologue: begin with a proverb or a saying; display one's humility; insist upon the duty to spread one's science; and remind the reader that it is necessary to avoid laziness (*eschiver oisiveté*).

Among these commonplaces (*topoï*), one of the richest is that of the *translatio studii et imperii*, the transmission of knowledge and power. Knowledge and power resided first in Greece. They went to Rome, then to France in a movement from east to west. And French texts show a desire for the movement to stop there and for this glory to remain in France. In the context of the Anglo-French war, there is more and more worry in the fourteenth century about seeing the *translatio* continue: seeing the power pass to England and the knowledge leave Paris for Oxford.

Another possible element of the exordium is the idea of a progress of knowledge. We run into this in the general prologue to Marie de France's *Lays*. The ancients wrote in a voluntarily obscure manner, thus permitting the moderns to "interpret the letter" (*gloser la letre*). This optimistic view sends us back to Bernard of Chartres' famous apothegm, recorded by John of Salisbury: "We are like dwarfs perched upon the shoulders of giants, and so able to see more and see farther than they" (Nous sommes des nains juchés sur des épaules de géants. Nous voyons ainsi davantage et plus loin qu'eux). This optimism is revived again in the fifteenth century. Martin le Franc expresses it in the *Champion des Dames*: "Science is like a deep well that the ancients explored. The new minds perfect what the old ones could not" (Science est comme ung puis parfont/Que les Anciens descouvrirent,/Ou les nouviaux engins parfont/Ce que les viellars ne parfirent; ll. 16345–16348). The verb *parfaire* (to perfect) is used to describe how they must finish what the ancients started; that is to say, to lead it to perfection. The idea of a continuity and a progress of knowledge had its partisans at the end of the Middle Ages, even if the opposite sentiment of decadence is more often represented.

Not all texts begin with a formal prologue. Rhetoric also teaches the possibility of starting in medias res. The prologue subsequently finds itself held back, shifted, or projected *en abyme* in the discourse of a character. In a consummate art of suspense and digression, the word that signals the prologue, *commencer* (to begin), appears in Villon's *Testament* a third of the way into the text: "For I wish to begin my testament" (Car commencer vueil à tester; l. 778) and "And here is the beginning" (Et vecy le commancement; l. 792). The prologue is out of place in Wace's *Roman de Rou* (it opens the third part), as well as in the *Chronique des ducs de Normandie* by Benoît de Sainte-Maure. It is *mis en abyme* in Chrétien de Troyes' *Knight of the Lion*, placed in the mouth of the character Calogrenant, who tells of his adventure.

How do medieval texts conclude? By this, I mean not dénouements that depend on the "matter" of the texts, but the formulae utilized to take leave of the listener or reader. The simplest, integrated or not into the text, is the [medieval] Latin word *explicit*. The formula in French that corresponds to this is "Ci falt" (Here ends): "Here ends the geste that Turoldus recounts" (Ci falt la geste que Turoldus declinet) at the end of the *Song of Roland*, or "Here ends the geste of the Bretons and the lineage of barons from which the Brut lineage comes" (Ci falt la geste des Bretuns/Et la lignee des baruns/Ki del lignage Bruti vindrent) in Wace's *Le Roman de Brut* (ll. 14859–14861). A variant is "Here finishes" (Ci fenist), as in "Here finishes Chrétien's work" (Ci fenist l'uevre Crestien) at the end of Chrétien de Troyes' *Cligés* and "Here finishes the *Dit dou Vergier*" (Ci fenist le *Dit dou Vergier*) at the end of said poem by Guillaume de Machaut. The conclusion is at times announced by a play on the rhyme *fin* understood with its two meanings: conclusion and perfection [*fin* in Old French means "fine" or "perfect" as well as "end"] of the heroes as of the text. Chrétien de Troyes does this in the *Knight of the Lion*. Speaking of Lunete, he writes, "Now that she has established an unending peace between the noble Sir Yvain and his dear and noble lady. Thus Chrétien brings to a close his romance of the Knight with the Lion" (Qu'ele a la pais faite sans fin/De mon signor Yvain le fin/Et de s'amic chicrc ct fine./Del chevalier al lion fine/Crestïens son romant issi; ll. 6801–6805). This game of *annominatio*, repetition under various forms of the word *fin*, a game of structural value, is found in works by other authors, such as Gautier de Coincy and Guillaume de Machaut. The *annominatio* on the word *fin*, its compounds and its derivatives, is developed in the same way over fourteen lines in the *Dit dou Vergier* (ll. 1269–1282). The figure of speech may hinge on a word that has a metadiscursive weight identical to *fin*, such as *chant* (song), *livre* (book), or *corde* (string). When the texts have a more developed epilogue, this is generally where the encoded name of the author is revealed. This presence of what the medieval French called an *engin* (clever device) is extremely characteristic of the end of Guillaume de Machaut's *dits*. The introductory formula for the *engin* is of the type: "he who wishes to know my name and my surname" (Qui savoir/Vorra mon nom et mon seurnom), followed by an indication of the literary maneuvers required to obtain it.

The endings are most often abrupt. "The romance is finished, I don't know any more about it" (Li romanz faut, je n'en sai plus), for example, ends one of the manuscripts of *Blancandin et l'Orgueilleuse d'Amour*. "Here I stop speaking, for I know no more about it" (Atant m'en tais, que plus n'en sai), Jean de Condé concludes his fabliau *Des braies le priestre*.

Sometimes the formula is lengthened with an indication: "whoever would say more about it would be lying" (qui en dirait plus, il mentirait), in Marie de France; or in Chrétien de Troyes, taking a poke at potential continuators. Sometimes the formula intends to tease the reader, as in the *Dit de la feste du Comte de Flandre* by Watriquet de Couvin: "Look for he who can say more about it" (Querez qui die le seurplus); or at the end of Guillaume de Machaut's *Fontaine amoureuse*: "Tell me, is this not a beautiful dream?" (Dites moy, fu ce bien songié?).

The abrupt closure is sometimes emphasized, contributing to the construction of the figure of the author or the constitution of the genre under which the text falls. The texts that are presented in the form of a dream put forward the brutal awakening of the dreamer for reasons that are internal and external to the dream: a drop of water falling from the tree as the god of love flies away in Guillaume de Machaut's *Dit dou Vergier*; a knock at the door, adopted by Christine de Pizan to end the *Chemin de Longue Etude*. François Villon invokes a circumstantial material reason to close the *Lais*: "I thought I could finish my work, but my ink was frozen and I found my candle blown out" (Je cuiday finer mon propos,/Mais mon ancrë estoit gelé/Et mon cierge trouvay soufflé; ll. 307–309); or a definitive reason when the author fictitiously has the end of his text coincide with the end of his life. Villon does this in the *Testament*: "Here ends the testament and poor Villon is finished" (Icy se clost le testament/Et finist du povre Villon; ll. 1996–1997). The author can use his weariness as an argument. Using this approach, Martial d'Auvergne creates a very beautiful *mise en abyme* to bring to a close his *Arrêts d'Amours*. In an intradiegetic way, the Presiding Judge announces that he is tired and turns the floor over to the court clerk. But the clerk has a soft voice, and the narrator cannot hear what he is saying. He adds: "And in addition my quill was quite tired, because I could not understand anything" (Et puis ma plume estoit fort lasse, / Par quoy n'eusse sceu rien comprendre), concluding for himself, "I must take my course elsewhere" (Ailleurs me fault prendre mon cours).

This posturing of the "elsewhere" is a complex figure. It can be found in prologues: it underlines the forced desire of the author and, in return, highlights the power of the command or of the request to which the author is submitting himself. A discreet, and therefore indirect, homage to the sponsor. Drouart la Vache explains at the beginning of his translation his decision to write of André le Chapelain's *De Amore*: "For I would not have put in my effort if I had not been begged for weeks to do it, for I have many other things to do" (Car je n'i meïsse ma paine, / S'on ne m'en priast de semaine, / Qu'assés ai autre chose affaire; ll. 13–15).

In a remarkable analysis, Christine de Pizan examines this tension between the patron's desire and the author's in the ballade that serves as the prologue to her book of *One Hundred Ballades of a Lover and His Lady*: "So I pray to God that I don't get tired of it, for I would much rather attend to something else of higher study, but I have been asked to do this by a gentle and noble person" (Or pry je a Dieu que n'en soye lassée / Car mieulx me pleust entendre a autre afaire / De trop greigneur estude, mais taussée / M'i a personne doulce et debonnaire). The formula can function inside the text as a simple commonplace of abridgement. The anonymous author of the romance *Floriant et Florete*, Christine de Pizan, at times, and Michault Taillevent use it in this way to cut short a tale or a description. In the epilogue, the expression is a way of taking leave that helps one understand to what extent the author has a global project, possibly even a mission, that goes beyond the work we have just read. Branch 9 of the *Roman de Renart* makes use of this process: "I would gladly have continued telling you the true adventures of Renart, but I am out of time, for another work is calling me. I want to undertake another narration in French, of a higher nature if it pleases God to help me" (De Renart encor vos contasse / En bon endroit, mes moi ne loist, / Qar autre besoigne me croist. / A autre romanz voil entendre / Ou l'en porra greignor sens prendre, / Se Dex plaist et se Dex m'amende; ll. 2200–2205). Guillaume de Machaut does the same thing. He concludes the *Jugement du Roi de Bohême* with these lines: "Here I will stop my tale and will make no more rhymes about it, for I have enough to write elsewhere" (Ci fineray/Ma matiere, ne plus n'en rimeray/Car autre part assez a rimer ay; ll. 2052–2054). In this same style, in her *Epistre à Pierre Col*, Christine de Pizan puts an end to her participation in the "*Querelle du* Roman de la Rose": "but I would rather work on other material that pleases me more" (mais mieulx me plaist exerciter en autre matiere mieulx a ma plaisance; ed. E. Hicks, p. 150).

The question of the commission and of the audience is present in the writing of the Middle Ages. The respective desires of author and reader enter into a rivalry at several levels. The naming of the work constitutes one of these points of discussion, or even contention.

The Question of the Title

The title is one of the subjects broached in the *Accessus ad auctores*; after the question of the author and before that of the subject matter and the intentions of the author and of the work. "The title . . . is a brief presentation of the work that follows" (Titulus . . . est brevis ostensio sequentis operis), Conrad de Hirsau says in his *Dialogus super auctores*. An *accessus* to the *Psychomachia* of [the third-century CE Roman poet] Prudentius offers a telling etymology: "Title comes in fact from the name of Titan; just as the latter illuminates the universe, the title must throw light on the work that follows it." The title, therefore, according to these authors, summarizes the work and orients the reader. Through the title, a link is made between the author and the reader. But not all medieval works have a title, and when it follows the formula "Here begins . . . " (Ici commence . . .), it is not always the choice of the author but may be an initiative taken by the scribe. Nevertheless, many authors make use of this pact with the reader. They then comment most often on the title that they have given to the work.

The title desired by the author may imply a rhetorical game, such as that played by Chrétien de Troyes in naming his third romance *The Knight of the Cart*: "Of the Knight of the cart Chrétien begins his book" (Del Chevalier de la charrete/Comance Crestïens son livre; ll. 24–25). The association of words creates an enigma and the name of the hero, Lancelot, does not appear until it is pronounced by the beloved lady, the queen, as we have seen. Similarly, he does not call the romance he is writing at the same time *Yvain*, but *The Knight of the Lion*; a paraphrase that puts forward the question of the identity of the hero and the fundamental link of the character and the animal: "Of the knight of the lion Chrétien has finished his romance here" (Del chevalier al lion fine/Crestïens son romant issi; ll. 6804–6805). It is a linguistic game for Marie de France, who states the title of her lays in several languages. Of *Bisclavret*, the werewolf, she writes, "In Breton his name is Bisclavret, the Normans call him Garou" (Bisclavret a nun en Bretan,/Garulf l'apelent li Norman; ll. 3–4), and of *Laustic*: "His name is 'Le Laustic,' I believe, in their country, that is, 'Le Rossignol' in French and 'The Nightingale' in good English" (Laustic a nun, ceo m'est vis,/si l'apelent en lur païs; ceo est russignol en Franceis/e nihtegale en dreit Engleis; ll. 3–6).

The double title can at times indicate a double polarization and consequently a double interpretation of the story. We find this, for example, in Marie de France's lay alternately called *The Wretched One* (*Chaitivel*) or the *Four Sorrows* (*Quatre Doels*), depending on whether we give our attention to the unfortunate surviving lover, for the former title, or to the fate of the four lovers, for the latter. The author concludes: "Each of the names is appropriate just as the matter requires it; but its usual name is *The Wretched One*" (Chescuns des nuns bien i afiert,/Kar la matire le requiert; Le Chaitivel a nun en us; ll. 235–237). The introduction of the idea of what is usual (*us*), customary, effectively illustrates this interaction between author and audience in the title. Guillaume de Machaut, in the fourteenth century, plays a similar game in some of his *dits*. In the *Voir-dit*, he refers to his preceding *dit*, that he has copied for his lady, under the double title *Morpheüs* or *La Fontaine amoureuse*: "I am sending you my book *Morpheus*, that is called *The Amorous Fountain*" (Je vous envoie mon livre de *Morpheus*, que on appelle *La Fontaine amoureuse;* letter 10). He concludes the *Dit de l'Alerion* by calling it, at the end of the work, *Le Dit des quatre oiseaux* (The Dit of the Four Birds). In each of the manuscripts, with one sole exception, the incipit announces: "Here begins the dit of the eaglet" (Ci commence le dit de l'alerion). As with Marie de France, the two titles focus on different aspects of the texts.

The author sometimes states that he prefers one particular title because it explains the work, is even the *reason* for the work. Reason is one of the meanings of the word *titre* (title) in Old French. The author has his reader question him rhetorically within the text. Guillaume de Lorris does this:

"And if somebody asks us what I want the romance that I am beginning to be called, let it be called the *Romance of the Rose*, where the art of Love is all enclosed" (Et se nule ne nus demande/comant je veil que li romanz/soit apelez que je comanz,/ce est li *Romanz de la Rose,*/ou l'art d'Amors est tote enclose; ll. 34–38). The formula can vary slightly. Jean de le Mote thus names his *Voie d'enfer*: "He who wishes to know and name this book will properly call it the *Path of Hell*" (Qui congnoistre et nommer vorra/Cestui libre, il l'appelera/Proprement la *Voie d'Infer*; ll. 37–39) or Jean Le Fèvre his *Livre de Leesce*: "I say that one will call it by its appropriate name *Book of Joy*" (Je dy que l'en l'appellera/Par droit nom *Livre de Leesce*). Note the standard and appropriate vocabulary: "properly" (*proprement*), "appropriately" (*par droit*). The poet justifies at times his desire. Guillaume de Machaut does this in his *Voir-dit:* "I want this text that I am writing for her to be called the *Voir-dit* [True Poem] because I will never lie in it" (Le *Voir Dit* veuil je qu'on appelle/Ce traitié que je fais pour elle,/Pour ce que ja n'i mentirai; ll. 518–520).

The naming by the author, be it serious or comical, can even be seen in terms of a baptism. Olivier de la Marche ends his *Triumphe des Dames* in this way: "And I, La Marche, full of goodwill, seeking virtues and pushing away sins, have baptized it the *Triumphe des dames*" (et je, La Marche, meült de bon voulloir,/querant vertus et reboutant les blasmes,/l'ay baptisié le *Triumphe des dames*). The author of the *Banquet du Boys* goes so far as to stage a conversation with the book: he interrogates it to learn its desire and, faced with its muteness, resolves himself to imposing the name: "Here is its name: it is the *Banquet of the Woods*" (Velà son nom: c'est le *Bancquet du Boys*). Why such an amused solemnity? The title may escape its author. François Villon describes this situation in the *Testament* apropos of his first text, the *Lais*, saying, "that some people, without my consent, have been determined to call a 'testament'" (qu'aucuns, sans mon consentement,/voulurent nommer "testament"; ll. 756–757). Villon pursues with a proverbial disenchanted reflection: "But what! we all say: 'nobody is master of his own property'" (Mais quoy! on dit communement: "ung chacun n'est maistre du scien"). He thus indirectly exonerates himself of all accusations of theft, since even intellectual property may be stolen. The new naming was significant. Villon's persona was sufficiently strong to encompass under his name both a "little" and a "big" testament, in an oblique and subversive wink at two other Testaments of a wholly different nature. The redaction of his work, a very rich editorial tradition, took this tack in the early sixteenth century.

For Whom Are They Writing?

Works intended for recitation or a public reading address the audience, as do those destined for private or individual reading. They are simply formulated differently. In each case, something specific is being asked of the audience, and this request can vary. The author may ask for benevolence (if it's a *captatio benevolentiae*); for physical or intellectual attention (silence in the context of a recitation), "Make peace" (Faites pais); or support: "Lend me your hearts and ears, for words that are not understood by the heart are lost completely" (Cuer et oroilles me rendés, Car parole oïe est perdue/S'ele n'est de cuer entendue), as Calogrenant puts it in *The Knight of the Lion* (ll. 150–152). He may be asking for an effort of interpretation when the text addresses the reader: "Here, Reader, fix your gaze well on the truth" (Aiguise ici, lecteur, ton regard sur le vrai), Dante warns in *Purgatory* (8.19).

The audience can be seen from a global point of view, including all who want to be amused or taught. The formula in the epic poem is of this type: "Would it please you to listen to a song of valor?" (Plaist vos oïr bone cançon vallant?), at the opening of the *Chanson d'Aspremont*; "Would it please you to hear a *chanson de geste*?" (Chanson de geste plaroit vos a entandre), as in the first line of the *Enfances Guillaume*. In the romance, the audience may be evoked as well. *La Manekine*, for example, begins with these lines: "Philippe de Rémi wants to compose a romance in which all those who hear it will take pleasure" (Phelippes de Remi ditier/Veut un roumans, u delitier/Se porront tuit cil qui l'orront).

Texts are written above all for the lords who can remunerate the storyteller. Rutebeuf lists at the beginning of the *Complainte d'Outremer*: "Emperor and king and count and duke and prince, to whom a man tells diverse romances to entertain you" (Empereour et roi et conte/Et duc et prince, a cui hom conte/Romans divers por vos esbatre).

The audience is usually defined by the nature of the prestigious person to whom the work is dedicated. Noble or not, the reader or the listener is thus indirectly qualified. A book of manners, the *Facet II*, in an address from the book to the reader, envisages the various divisions of the audience from a sociological point of view. It opposes, according to class: nobles and villeins (serfs); according to status: clerics and laymen; according to age: the young and the old. But the audience can also be called upon in its imaginary or symbolic dimension. Texts may address lovers in the same way that they do knights, clerics or merchants. Social and moral categories are mixed together. In the *Dit du Florin*, Jean Froissart enumerates all those who are loved by money, which is unfortunately not the case for him, and he lists: "The nobles and the well dressed, the lovers, the happy, the pilgrims, the merchants" (Les nobles et les orfrisiés,/Les amourous, les envoisiés,/Les pelerins, les marchëans; ll. 27–29). Here he includes lovers in the estates of the world.

There are, indeed, numerous texts that claim to address this multiform, yet ideologically coherent, category. Thomas d'Angleterre concludes his *Tristan* with the formula: "Here Thomas finishes his text and salutes all lovers" (Tumas fine ci sun escrit:/A tuz amanz saluz i dit; ll. 820–821). Hue de Rotelande does the same thing in *Ipomedon*: "To all lovers, Ipomedon sends greetings in this romance by Hue de Rotelande" (Ipomedon a tuz amanz/Mande saluz en cest romanz/Par cest Hue de Rotelande; ll. 10559–10561). Jean de Meun addresses lovers in the *Romance of the Rose*: "Here I ask of you, lords in love" (Si vos pri, seigneur amoreus).

Combining the moral and the social, one public is unanimously rejected: the villeins. This theme traverses the Middle Ages. The author of the *Roman de Thèbes* affirms: "May those who are not clerics or knights save themselves the trouble of listening to me for they are as suited to listening as a donkey is to playing the harp" (Or s'en tesent de cest mestier,/se ne sont clerc ou chevalier,/car ausi puent escouter/conme li asnes a harper; ll. 13–16). Jean Froissart echoes this in the *Joli Buisson de Jonece*: "It is not at all for the serfs" (Ce n'est mie pour les villains; l. 41). Slanderers, those who do not know how to listen with their hearts, are also excluded, as well as those who disturb the recitation or the reading. Philippe de Rémi reminds us of this firmly at the beginning of *La Manekine*: "It is an act that is neither courtly nor wise to trouble a storyteller" (Ce n'est courtoizie ne sen/De nul conteeur destourber; ll. 10–11). In his forceful language, Gautier de Coinci does likewise at the opening of the miracle *D'un clerc* (Of a Cleric): "To whom it displeases, without delay, may he withdraw, may he leave" (Cui il anuit, tout sanz delaie/Traie se arriere, si s'en voise; ll. 10–11). And he insists: "May he leave, may he leave" (Voist s'en, voist s'en).

The audience can also be envisioned in a personal or familial way. The book then plays the double game of addressing first this close audience and of aiming at the general public—the listener or reader—in the background. In the field of love and lovers, this gives rise to books that declare that they were written for the poet's lady, as a form of confession, declaration, or homage. This is done, to give a few examples, by Thibaut, the author of the *Roman de la Poire*; the author of the *Roman du Castelain de Couci et de la Dame de Fayel*; and Guillaume de Machaut in his *Voirdit*. A type of romance thus emerges that is fictitiously interactive, where the narrator's decision to return to and find a way to conclude his work is declared to be dependent upon his lady's acceptance of his love. Renaut de Beaujeu does this in the *Bel Inconnu*: "When it pleases you, say so, or he will ever more be silent" (Quant vos plaira, dira avant,/U il se taira ore a tant; ll. 6253–6254). Between the two loves, the queen and the fairy, Renaut chooses the ideologically "correct" solution for his hero: marriage. It is up to his lady to bring him back to the task so that love, ignoring social norms—the love of the fairy—triumphs. In the didactic domain, an author can claim to write for her son, as Christine de Pizan does in her *Enseignements moraux*. The Lyonnais merchant François Garin likewise asserts this in his *Complainte*. Geoffroi de la Tour Landry writes for his daughters; the author of the *Mesnagier de Paris*, for his wife; Jacques d'Ableiges, in his *Grand Coutumier de France*, for his nephews. Saint Louis, King Louis IX himself, bequeathed an *Enseignements à son fils* (Teachings for His Son) written in French to the future Philippe III and to his daughter Isabelle.

The Female Audience

Texts pay particular attention to the figure of the female listener or the female reader. Ladies, noble ladies, constitute a group mentioned separately in the romances. Describing King Arthur's court in *The Knight of the Cart*, Chrétien de Troyes focuses on this group: "A great number of beautiful courtly ladies, skilful at conversing in French" (mainte bele dame cortoise/bien parlant en lengue françoise; ll. 39–40). In *Erec and*

Enide, he depicts ladies composing poetry, a lay, "The Joy of the Court," as a reaction to a supernatural (*merveilleux*) episode: "And ladies composed a lay and called it the Joy of the Court" (Et les dames un lai troverent/Que le Lai de Joie apelerent; ll. 6179–6180), adding, to create an effect of realism: "But this lay is hardly known" (Mais n'est gaires li laiz seüz). One goes to specific places of hearing to be entertained in the company of ladies, to tell them of feats of war or to listen to stories: ladies' chambers. A scene from Jean Renart's romance of the *Escoufle* speaks of such moments of relaxation for men, where ladies and stories commingle. The count of Saint-Gilles spends time with his lady's maids to "eat fruits and relax" (mangier son fruit et aaisier; l. 7024). An intimate scene: "He undresses to scratch, leaving nothing on but his breeches" (Il se despoille por grater,/Et n'i laisse riens a oster/Fors ses braies). This brings to mind scenes of delousing in other civilizations, but also instances of storytelling. He rests his head on the lap of Aelis, the heroine, who hides her identity and has him tell her of a hunting party that took place that very day, enabling the identification of the hero. Telling of a tournament, the romance *Gliglois* alludes to these ladies' chambers where fiction intersected with real life. So does Jean de Joinville in his *Life of Saint Louis,* where he reports the words of his cousin Jean II de Nesle, comte de Soissons, at the battle of Mansoura [in Egypt, where King Louis and his men were defeated and captured by the Mameluks in 1250]: "We shall speak again of this day, between you and me, in the ladies' chambers" (encore en parlerons nous entre vous et moy de ceste journee es chambres des dames; § 242). In Guillaume de Machaut's *Jugement du Roi de Navarre,* Reason reproaches the poet for the weakness of his arguments against women. She calls his words "frivolous," adding: "They are good for telling in the [lady's] chamber" (Belles sont a conter en chambre; l. 3991). The irony expressed is that the arguments against women are good for ladies' chambers, where men can brag and the recital of fiction blossoms.

Another place specifically for listening is what Christine de Pizan calls the table of queens. In her letter to Jean de Montreuil, she criticizes the *Romance of the Rose,* especially its ending, the deflowering of the Rose, as unsuitable for reading in the presence of women: "So why praise a text that no one will dare read or tell in a proper setting—at the table of queens, princesses, or decent bourgeois ladies?" (Et dont que fait a louer lecture qui n'osera estre leue ne parlee en propre forme a la table des roynes, des princesses et des vaillans preudefemmes? p. 20). For both positive and negative reasons, a female audience stands out, in fiction as in life. Translations are very specifically dedicated to ladies, the general supposition being that women do not know how to read Latin. The author of *l'Isopet I*, a collection of fables from the very end of the thirteenth century, confides:

> Pour les dammes tant seulement
> L'ai du latin trait en rommant
> Exquelles excellent clergie,
> Ne trés eminent n'affiert mie
>
> (I translated it from Latin to French for the ladies only, in whom an excellent and very eminent culture is not appropriate).
>
> (*EPILOGUE*, ll. 15–18)

This bias was still very much alive at the beginning of the sixteenth century. Jean Lemaire de Belges concludes book 3 of his *Illustrations de Gaule et Singularitez de Troye* with these words: "And for this, lords, if the ladies who by chance read or hear a reading of this book were to be at times bothered or angry to find so much Latin mixed in among the French, I count on your good means to justify myself" (Et pour ce, seigneurs, si les dames qui d'aventure liront ou orront lire ce livre, estoient quelque fois ennuyees et fachees de trouver tant de Latin entremeslé parmy le François: je pourray par vostre bon moyen, trouver lieu d'excuse; p. 469). And Lemaire invokes the practice of preachers "who often cite a lot of Latin, in their sermons, to the village females, to corroborate and persuade that which they want to tell the people" (lesquelz alleguent souvent beaucoup de latin, en leurs sermons, aux femmelettes de village, pour corroborer et persuader ce qu'ilz veullent donner à entendre au peuple). In 1504, Antoine Du Four explains the redaction in French of his work, *Les Vies des femmes célèbres*, based on Boccaccio's *De mulieribus claris*, which he is writing for Anne de Bretagne, in this way: "And considering that most noble ladies of France do not understand Latin" (Et considéré que la plupart des nobles dames de France ne entendent le langage latin . . .).

Religious, moral teachings are offered to ladies. Durand de Champagne's *Speculum dominarum*, composed for Joan of Navarre, the wife of Philip the Fair, was translated twice into French and circulated in this form. Watriquet de Couvin dedicated an allegorical poem entitled *Miroir aux dames* (Mirror to the Ladies) to Charles the Fair's third wife, Jeanne d'Evreux, in 1325. The Carthusian Frère Robert wrote his *Chastel perilleux* for a (female) cousin of his. One Robert, perhaps the same, composed a *Trésor de l'âme* for his mother and "all Christians."

The management of estates was also addressed: Robert Grosseteste [c. 1175–1253; bishop of Lincoln in England] wrote a treatise on the subject, *Les Reulles Saint Robert,* for the countess of Lincoln. Feminine taste can be historically deduced from queens' libraries, which include collections of fables in French, in addition to covering the religious and didactic fields already mentioned. Examples include the libraries of Philip the Bold's second wife, Maria of Brabant; Clementia of Hungary [Clémence d'Anjou], second wife of King Louis X [of France] the Stubborn; and Jeanne d'Evreux, widow of King Charles IV the Fair. In the *Livre des trois vertus*, Christine de Pizan enjoins the governess of a young princess to tell her "from time to time fables and stories that are told to children" (aucunes foiz des fables et des comptes que on dit a enfans; 1.24).

Some authors explicitly specify this feminine taste in literary terms. Denis Piramus, in *La vie saint Edmund le rei*, says: "Lays ordinarily please women" (Les lais solent as dames pleire). Authors may also dream of specific places of storytelling (and listening), whose formulation expresses their poetics. The troubadour Guiraut de Bornelh, who extols *trobar leu* (composing clearly) in opposition to *trobar clus* (deliberately composing obscurely), wishes to hear his songs in the mouths of the women carrying water (*porteuses d'eau*) at the fountain.

CHAPTER FOUR

The Work and Its Milieux

B EHIND THE ACKNOWLEDGED AUDIENCE, the one inscribed within the works, real audiences exist and they are variously stratified. This chapter will indicate a few of the directions that a sociological analysis could take. Three large social fields concern both producers and consumers of literature, with different emphases according to the periods: the church, the courts, and, starting in the thirteenth century, the city.

The Church and the University

The Church, in other words, the world of the clerics, was distinguished by the use of Latin, but communicated in French as well for the purposes of teaching, preaching, and diffusing knowledge. The creation of the University of Paris, whose first privileges were granted by Philip Augustus in 1200 and confirmed by Pope Innocent II in 1215, played an essential role in the structuring of the milieu of scholarly readers who, through translation from Latin to French, passed on theological, philosophical, and technical knowledge. The shift to French essentially concerned the Bible and took on various forms: glosses, partial adaptations in verse and in prose, and complete translations as early as 1250. Knowledge was spread in French by means of translations. There were translations of books such as the *Commencement de sapience* (Beginning of Wisdom) [an astrological treatise by Abraham ibn Ezra; 1089?–1164], translated from Hebrew by Hagin in 1273; translations of Arabic medical texts from Latin versions, such as the *Chirurgie* (Surgery) by Albucasis (Abu Al-Qasim), translated into French from Gerard of Cremona's Latin version; and translations from Latin of Aristotle's writings.

The world of the university became a center for debates. Rivalry between the universities of Orléans and Paris spurred arguments such as the so-called quarrel between the Ancients and the Moderns, giving rise to Henry d'Andeli's *Battle of the Seven Arts*. Orléans argued for grammar and the study of the classical authors, Paris for logic and the study of Aristotle, as well as opposition to the mendicant orders, fueled by [the theologian] Guillaume de Saint-Amour in Latin and [the poet] Rutebeuf in French.

The Courts

Courts were dominated by wealthy patrons. Some were quite famous and constituted veritable literary centers, attracting jongleurs and enrolling minstrels. One of the most famous was the court of Henry II of England and Eleanor of Aquitaine. Queen Eleanor was also an independent patron in her own right. Very often due to familial ties, the relations between these courts, relations of emulation and rivalry, contributed to the production and the diffusion of works. The enumeration by an author of his successive patrons became a more and more frequent occurrence in prologues. The names of these people of high rank validated the work and functioned as a means of publicity, arousing new patrons or even prompting sons to be as generous as their fathers. Guiot de Provins, in his *Bible Guiot* (c. 1206), a text that militates against the world of the courts and the clergy, strings together the names of his protectors: Richard the Lionheart; Comte Henri I of Champagne, Peter II of Aragon and his brother Ramon Berenguer of Provence; Frederick I Barbarossa. Jean Froissart does likewise in the *Joli Buisson de Jonece* [1373], citing thirty or so names, including Edward III of England's wife, Philippa of Hainaut, and her entourage; Charles V [of France]; Wenceslaus of Bohemia; Louis, Jean, and Guy de Blois; Amadeus VI, count of Savoy; Peter I de Lusignan, king of Cyprus; and the king of Scotland. This small sampling gives an idea of the diversity of the courts and sponsors that he managed to serve.

The City

Some cities play a preponderant role in literature, particularly—for the thirteenth century—the city of Arras. The development of theater is tied to this city with two major authors: Jean Bodel (died in 1210) and his *Jeu de saint Nicolas* (Play of St. Nicholas), and Adam de la Halle (died in 1290) and *Le Jeu de la Feuillée* (Play of the Greensward). Theatrical staging remained an activity of the city throughout the medieval period, with the development of miracle and mystery plays in the fourteenth and fifteenth centuries. The complex relations between the royal power and the cities were embodied in a specific genre of shows, the *Entrées royales*. At the same time, a new type of text, *dits* of trades like *Crieries de Paris* and Rutebeuf's *Dit de l'Herberie* (Tale of the Herb Market), captured the noises and voices of the city. Founded on the enumeration, on the esthetic of the list, they are imbued with urban traffic and reproduce the animation of the streets, the practices of merchants and salesmen. This urban poetry was developed by Eustache Deschamps in the fourteenth century and in the fifteenth century by François Villon. These authors conceived of the city as a network that brought together pleasures and dangers, taverns and steam rooms. The poetry of the city was to have a long future. Literary criticism has determined that the "old book" Guillaume Apollinaire had under his arm when he strolled along the edges of the Seine in the early twentieth century was Gaston Paris and Ernets Langlois' *Chrestomathie du moyen âge*. And consider Léon-Paul Fargue's *Piéton de Paris*, Louis Aragon's *Paysan de Paris*, or Georges Perec's attempt to exhaustively describe a particular Parisian location.

With the promotion of the city, a new type of patron arose, the rich merchant. In the fourteenth century, the great Parisian goldsmith Simon de Lille was the protector of Jean de le Mote, who names him three times and pays homage to him in the *Parfait du Paon*. Jean de le Mote says of him what Chrétien de Troyes says of Marie de Champagne: "For my master de Lille, who is called Simon, gave me the matter and the introduction" (Car mon maistre de Lille, c'on apelle Symon,/M'a donné la matere et l'introduction; ll. 51–52). But he adds practical details as well. Simon "gives to me food and room and a scribe so that I may make beautiful compositions; I do not serve him in any other way" (me livre vivre, chambre et clerc escrisant/Pour faire li biax dis; d'el ne le vois servant; ll. 1456–1457). The poet's material needs are met by the patron, but for very specific intellectual work, a new source of pride for these authors. They are no longer seen as multitalented entertainers.

Along the same lines, Laurent de Premierfait was protected by two important officials under Charles VI: Jean Chanteprime, controller of finances, who hosted him while he finished his translation of Boccaccio's

De Casibus; and, after the death of Chanteprime, Bureau de Dampmar-
tin, the king's treasurer, under whose roof he translated the *Decameron*
according to an economical process that he explains. Recalling the double
translation that was necessary in order to translate the *Decameron* first
from Florentine into Latin and then from Latin into French, he adds for
the attention of Bureau: "all the remuneration for the labor and the ex-
pense of said book has since been liberally done and administered by you
in that you are the true and only mediator by whom the said book has
thus been compiled and written in two languages" (toute la retribucion
du labour et de la despence dudit livre depuis a esté liberalement par vous
faicte et administree en tant que vous estes le vray et seul mediateur par
qui ledit livre est ainsi compilé et escript en deux langaiges; p. 4).

Fraternal Networks

The dependence that bound a poet to a patron was personal, like feudal allegiance, but ties—of friendship, of rivalry, of play—also existed
between poets. Marcabru sends the song "I want to begin courteously"
(Cortezament vuelh comensar) to Jaufre Rudel "overseas" (*ultra mar*).
Peire d'Alvernhe and the Monk of Montaudon draw ironic portraits
of their colleagues, but include themselves in the final stanza in these
"literary galleries." In Arras, in the thirteenth century, the *jeu-parti*—a
dialogue in stanzas between two poets who divided a question, one de-
fending the "pros" and the other the "cons"—created a rivalry between
poets, no matter their social class. A medieval poetic society, called the
Puy, was created to hold contests. Each year a president was elected and
was given the title *prince du Puy*. Jehan Bretel, a rich bourgeois who
was prince of the Puy, exchanged a large number of *partures* (this type
of dialogue)—we can count eighty-nine—with twenty or so other poets
of all conditions. This horizontal network developed at the end of the
Middle Ages, taking two forms: happy, fraternal bacchic and goliardic
[satirical versifying] societies, friends *in praesentia* with whom one celebrated; and circles of serious humanists, friends *in absentia* to whom
one wrote. Both bear witness to an immense literary vitality, to a taste for
writing and a pleasure in the letters.

   The first network placed itself under the sign of joy and wine. Joyous
drinkers and happy lads got together under the label of the *galois*, men

of pleasure or joy (the word *gal* means joy), of the *frequantans* (regulars) of the tavern. Eustache Deschamps' *Charte des bons enfans de Vertus en Champagne*, dated August 1372, gives testimony to this. The scholarly exchanges took place at the level of violent or friendly disputes for mastery, the pursuit of literary recognition. "Orators and poets are not to be found outside of Italy" (Extra Italiam oratores et poetas non querendos), the Italian poet laureate Petrarch asserted (*Seniles* 9.1), and French humanists like Anseau Choquart and Jean de Hesdin took up the challenge. In French rather than in Latin, the exchange of ballades between Philippe de Vitry, Jean de le Mote, and Jean Campion created a way of speaking about poetry under the colors of mythology, celebrating the inspiration received from the Muses. Philippe de Vitry, Petrarch's friend, accused Jean de le Mote of not knowing how to make Pegasus fly. Christine de Pizan sent an *Epistre* to Eustache Deschamps who, in turn, responded to her with high praise, saying. "O muse, whose eloquence rivals the nine [Muses]" (Muse eloquent entre les IX). Philippe de Mézières, who spent three years in Venice, translated his friend Petrarch's Latin version of the final novella of Boccaccio's *Decameron*, the story of Griselda, into French. The network of friends and of exchanges was dense and gave shape to milieus and places.

The Literary Provinces

In the Middle Ages, poetry was viewed from a geographical standpoint, linked with the poet's place of origin or love affairs. Well-read medieval milieus combined social stratification with perceptions of literary territories or regions. There was, for example, the Provence of Peire Vidal, from Toulouse, the air that he breathed in from the country "between [the] Rhône and Vence, enclosed by the sea and the Durance," a geographical definition but also a political one, as has been shown by Fredrick Cheyette. Gace Brulé, while he was in Brittany, remembered "sweet Champagne" by the grace of the birds, "birds of [his] country" (des oisillons de [s]on pays). "Sweet" (*Doux*) is a laudatory qualifier of strong affectivity, as is shown by the mentions of "sweet France" in the *chanson de geste*. Champagne played an eminent part in medieval French literature on account of the court of Comte Henri I and Marie of Champagne, which produced the prince-poet Thibaut IV. Gautier d'Epinal, a knight from Lorraine and a poet, regretted not being Champenois.

Praise for Champagne continued in the fourteenth century. In his ballade entitled in the manuscript *Des Meurs et condicions des Champainoys* (Of the manners and [Social] Conditions of the Champenois; 8: 177–178), Eustache Deschamps names five of these who are "adept at writing": Petrus Comestor, Saincte More (although he gets the name wrong, he is referring here to the author of *Ovide moralisé*), Philippe de Vitry, Guillaume de Machaut, and Nicolas de Clamanges. In other ballades, Deschamps develops a double image contrasting Brie, which he execrates, and Champagne, which he showers with praise. He lauds in particular his native town, Vertus, the well-named.

Lorraine, of which Gautier d'Epinal regretted being a native, is nevertheless praised in the *Romance of the Rose*. The jongleurs and the minstrels encountered by the dreamer inside the garden have in their repertory "airs from Lorraine because more beautiful songs are made in Lorraine than in any other kingdom" (notes lohorenges / por ce c'on fet en Loheraigne / plus beles notes qu'en nul raigne). The poetic and musical repertories cited in the works mention a classification that sounds like a list of "specialties" of different provinces or countries. In *Galeran de Bretagne*, the godfather of the young girl, Frêne, teaches her: "All of the Saracen melodies, the songs of Gascony, of the Ile de France, of Lorraine and the Breton lays" (Toute notes sarrasinoises, / Chançons gascoignes et françoises, / Loerraines, et laiz bretons). Continuing the debate tradition, Guillaume Cretin, at the turn of the sixteenth century, enters into the Debate over Women (*La Querelle des Dames*) by creating a subgenre: the quarrel of the Ladies of Paris and Lyon. On behalf of the ladies of Paris, he addresses a "poetic composition to the bourgeois of Lyon," who answer him, initiating a satirical exchange. This rivalry, and the vitality of the literary milieu, foretold a bright literary future for Lyon in the sixteenth century.

The Field of Literature

The Subject Matter

W HAT DID FRENCH AUTHORS write about in the Middle Ages? What
is the subject matter [*la matière*] of their texts? This is one part
of the questions raised by the *accessus*.[1] Etymologically, the French word
matière signifies the construction material used to make something, its
planking (*merrain*), and the people of the Middle Ages heard in it, as did
Isidore of Seville, an echo of the word *mère* ("mother"). Practicing what
Rémy de Gourmont calls a "mystical pun," at times some even read in it
a crasis—that is, a combination—of the words *mater* and *Maria*. In one
of her *Louanges de Sancta Maria* (Praises of Holy Mary), Hildegard von
Bingen finds a link between God's creation of the world starting with a
prima materia (first matter) and his re-creation thanks to Mary, *lucida
materia* (clear matter) who carried the Christ child, the instrument of the
redemption. According to medieval theories of the time, borrowed from
Aristotle, matter is that which is not yet organized by a form: in the domain of literary creation, subject matter is what sets in motion, or makes
possible, the process of writing.

A series of terms can be substituted for "subject matter" with reference
to the content of a work. They are borrowed from the field of philosophy,
like "substance," or from the field of language, like "reason," "subject"
[*propos*], and "theme." The very common word "subject" [*sujet*] was
only rarely used in this sense during the Middle Ages. The Anglo-Norman
author Pierre of Fetcham uses it, but with a gloss, which indicates its un-
usual character: in his *Lumere as Lais* he speaks of "The subject of this
book, or the matter" (Le suget de cest livere, ou la matire; l. 553). "Matter" is therefore the essential term, and this designation, rather than the
use of the word "subject," philosophically steers all medieval thought.
"Matter" puts the accent on the material, the dough, that is going to be
shaped by the forms.

The term is often qualified. Subject matter is defined both from a moral point of view—it may be either good or bad—and from an esthetic point of view, the two aspects being linked. "The matter is sweet and beautiful" (La matiere est douce et belle), says the thirteenth-century French translator of the *Evangiles des Domées*. The two criteria constitute one of the justifications of writing: "For it is a joy to make a good work from matter that will last forever" (Car joie est de bon oevre faite/De matire qui touz jours dure), writes Raoul de Houdenc in the prologue of his romance *Méraugis de Portlesguez* (ll. 6–7, Vienna MS). Resulting from this is a duty of the author with regard to the matter. Marie de France opens the *Lai de Guigemar*, her first lay, with these lines: "Whoever has good material for a story is grieved if the tale is not well told" (Ki de bone matire traite,/mult li peise, se bien n'est faite). The top qualities for a matter are: its originality, "The matter is good and new" (La matire est bonne et neuve; *Romance of the Rose*, l. 39); its refinement, "The matter is good and fine" (La matire en est bone et fine; *Le Roman de la Poire*, l. 388); and its weight. Jean Froissart speaks of his "high and noble matter"(*haulte et noble matiere*) at the opening of the fourth book of his *Chronicles*.

The nature of the subject matter implies a choice of form, verse or prose, and necessitates a certain medium, Latin or French. In addressing questions of theology in his *Champion des dames*, Martin le Franc comments, "And the matter is of weight, demanding more prose than verse" (Si est la matiere pesant,/Plus requerant prose que rime; ll. 21273–21274). He even specifies, "Thus it would be better to speak in Latin than in the common language" (Aussi en deubt on mieulz parler/En latin qu'en commun langage; ll. 21281–21282).

Choosing Subject Matter

The decision to write may originate from one of three sources: the patron, as we have already seen, the author, and, in a way that may seem paradoxical, the subject matter itself. As far as the author is concerned, the most scholarly remind themselves of Horace's precept: "You who write, choose a matter that's proportionate to your strengths" (Sumite materiam vestris, qui scribitis, aequam/Viribus . . . ; *Ars poetica*, ll. 38–39). This is what Dante is saying in his essay *De vulgari eloquentia* (On Eloquence in the Vernacular) "I say therefore that each must equal the weight of his matter to [the strength of] his own shoulders, for fear that the latter being too weighted down, he will end up tripping in the mud" (2.4.4).

Likewise, in the prologue of his *Condamnation de Banquet*, Nicolas de La Chesnaye writes: "O you who write or who would get involved in compiling some works, choose a matter that is not too high, nor too difficult, but that is simply appropriate to the power and capacity of your understanding" (O vous qui escrivez ou qui vous meslez de compiler aucunes oeuvres, eslisez matiere qui ne soit trop haulte ne trop difficille, mais soit seullement convenable a la puissance et capacité de vostre entendement). La Chesnaye puts this principle into perspective, however, by recalling the role of the commission in the choice of the matter: "However much Horace wrote in his [*Ars poetica*]. . . the author or composer of such works may nevertheless often be so strongly required and solicited . . ." (Combien que Orace en sa Poeterie ait escript . . . ce neantmoins, l'acteur ou compositeur de telles oeuvres peut souventesfois estre si fort requis et sollicité. . .).[2] He thus introduces the topos of humility.

The third form has the matter voluntarily giving itself over to the will of the author with a certain amount of urgency. This is the position taken by Georges Chastellain in his *Chronique*. Subject matters present themselves to him "lamenting their own lack of felicity" (plaintives de leur propre infélicité) and, he says, "do not cease to collide with my quill by way of a reminder" (ne cessent de hurter à ma plume par manière de ramentevance; *Oeuvres,* ed. Kervyn de Lettenhove, 3:388). Elsewhere, he calls attention to what seem to him to be digressions arising not from the requirements of the subject matter but from his own pleasure. Describing the marvels of Rouen, he says: "I included them here, not by any necessity to my matter, but out of admiration for the thing" (sy les ay mises, non pas par nécessité de ma matière, mais par admiration de la chose; ibid., 359).

The matter has laws and rights. To justify themselves or to apologize, the authors resort to formulae of this type: "For the matter requires it" (Kar la matire le requiert; Marie de France, the *Lai du Chaitivel*, l. 236); "For this was required by the matter" (Que ce requeroit la matire; Jean de Meun, *The Romance of the Rose*, l. 15143); or "It does not suit my matter" (Il n'afiert pas a ma matere; Gautier d'Arras, *Eracle*, l. 5088). The matter has a meaning, it has a unity. Godefroy de Lagny, who completed *The Knight of the Cart* at the request of Chrétien de Troyes, and who did not want to deal with Meleagant's sister, wrote:

> Mes n'an vuel feire mancion,
> Car n'afiert pas a ma matire
> Que ci androit an doie dire,
> Ne je ne la vuel boceier
> Ne corronpre ne forceier,
> Mes mener boen chemin et droit   (ll. 6246–6251)

> (I do not wish to speak further of her now, however, since it is not part of my story to tell of her at this point, and I do not want to inflate or confuse or alter my story, but develop it in a proper and straightforward manner; p. 284)

He concludes the work with these words: "My lords, if I were to tell any more, I would be going beyond my matter" (Seignor, se j'avant an disoie,/Ce seroit oltre la matire; ll. 7098–7099).

Medieval Taxonomies

The subject matters are diverse. They are defined in relation to or in comparison with one another: "The matter is from God and from weapons and from love" (Li matere est de Dieu et d'armes et d'amour; l. 10) says Adam de la Halle in his *Chanson du roi de Sicile*, designating large fields of medieval literature. Some authors elaborate authoritarian classifications. Jean Bodel does this, for the narrative domain, in the prologue to his *Song of the Saxons* (*Chanson des Saisnes*):

> N'en sont que trois materes a nul home vivant:
> De France et de Bretaigne et de Ronme la grant   (ll. 6–7)

> (There are but three matters for any living man: of France and of Brittany and of Rome the great.)

In this way, he distinguishes the matter of France, which refers to the domain of the *chanson de geste*; the matter of Brittany, meaning by this the Arthurian romances; and the matter of Rome, the classical romances. He characterizes these fields: "The tales of Brittany are futile and pleasant, those of Rome full of wisdom and instructive, those of France, true, as is seen every day" (Li conte de Bretaigne si sont vain et plaisant,/Et cil de Ronme sage et de sens aprendant,/Cil de France sont voir chascun jour aparant; ll. 9–11).

The panorama is partial but shows well how, for a man of the Middle Ages, the texts were also grouped together by their mode of action on the audience. The categories of thought are pleasure, usefulness, and truth. The anonymous thirteenth-century author of an Arthurian romance, *Durmart le Galois* (Durmart of Wales), uses the same classification to praise his hero whose renown endures:

> Li bons rois Artur est fenis,
> Mais encore dure ses pris,
> Et de Charlemaine ensement
> Parolent encore la gent,
> Et d'Alixandre, ce savons,
> Dure encore li grans renons   (ll. 15939–15944)

(Good King Arthur is no longer but his worth still endures; the people, in the same way, still speak of Charlemagne; as for Alexander, we know well, his great renown still endures).

From the combination of matters, great fields identified by the authors or their audience (God, weapons, love); forms (prose and verse, song and *dit*); and modes of action (wisdom and pleasure, fable and story), come what we may call "genres."

Singing of Feats (*Gestes*)

In the fabliau of the *Deux bordeors ribauz* (The Two Ribald Braggarts), the two braggarts throw their repertoires in each other's faces. In both cases, they are lists of *chansons de geste*. The first, who proclaims, "For I know of chanson de geste" (Car ge sai de chançon de geste; l. 64), enumerates a dozen of them and concludes: "There is not a song in the whole world that I do not know innately" (Il n'est chançon en tot le mont/Que je ne saiche par nature; ll. 100–101). The second replies to him with an enumeration just as abundant concluding, "All the *chansons de geste* that you know how to tell, I know how to tell and sing by heart" (De totes les chançons de geste / Que tu sauroies aconter / Sai ge par cuer dire et conter; ll. 320–322).

The *chanson de geste* (epic poem) constitutes an important genre of medieval literature and the authors started fairly quickly to classify the matters that gave rise to these songs. In the prologue to his song *Girart de Vienne*, Bertrand de Bar-sur-Aube asserts: "There have been only three *gestes* [or cycles] in well-defended France" (N'ot que trois gestes en France la garnie; l. 11). The desire to define the scope of the matters is the same as that displayed by Jean Bodel—both write at the turn of the twelfth century—but for Bertrand it is limited to the domain of the *geste*. He distinguishes, thus, three *gestes:* the *geste* of the king, concerning Charlemagne or the kings of France; the *geste* of Doon de Mayence, or the cycle of the traitorous barons (Bertrand makes Doon the ancestor of Ganelon, mixing rebellious heroes with traitorous ones); and the *geste* of *Garin de Monglane*, also known as the "William of Orange cycle," whose family emblematizes services rendered to the king of France and to Christianity.

This three-way division of the epic matter is found elsewhere with variants in the naming of the *gestes*. The *geste* of the king is sometimes called the "*geste* of Pepin and of the angel" by the thirteenth-century poem about *Doon de Mayence*, a title that one already comes across in a Saintongeais chronicle from the beginning of the same century that affirms: "There are three *gestes* in France, one about Pepin and the angel" (Tres gestes ot en France, l'una de Pepin et de l'angre). Other texts enumerate the *chansons de geste*, sorting the matter for the geste of kings chronologically. They distinguish, then, between Merovingian and Carolingian epics. This is done in the *Chanson de Guillaume* (Song of William) in a reference to the repertory of a jongleur:

> Et de la geste li set dire les chançuns,
> De Clodoveu, le premier empereur
> Que en duce France creeit en Deu, nostre seignur,
> Et de sun fiz Flovent le poigneür,
> Ki laissad de dulce France l'onur,
> E de tuz les reis qui furent de valur
> Tresque a Pepin, le petit poigneür,
> Et de Charlemaigne et de Rollant, sun nevou,

De Girard de Viane et de Oliver, qui fu tant prouz:
Cil furent si parent e sis ancesur.   (ll. 1261–1270)

(And he knows something of the *geste* of Clovis, the first emperor
who in sweet France believed in God, our lord, and of his son Flovent
Le Poigneur, who left sweet France with honor, and of all of the kings
who were worthy all the way to Pepin, the Little Poigneur, and of
Charlemagne and of Roland, his nephew, of Girard de Vienne and of
Olivier, who was so valiant: these were his family and his ancestors.)

Finally, some *chansons de geste* are organized around the theme of
the crusade against the Saracens, taking for pivotal hero Godefroy de
Bouillon. The crusade against the Albigensians also gave rise to *chansons*.
Starting in the fourteenth century, the classics supplied subject matter for
the epic. Thus, in 1343, Nicholas of Verona used passages from the *Faits
des Romains* as a guide in composing his *Pharsale*. There had always been
close ties between chronicles and epics. Girart d'Amiens' *Charlemagne* is
a reworking of the *Grandes Chroniques de France*.

Tales About Arthur

Next to the matter of France, Jean Bodel singles out the matter of Brittany, which he places in the category of fiction and entertainment. Likewise, the first of the *deux bordeors ribauz*, after having affirmed his talent
as a singer of gestes, proclaims: "I know adventure romances, those of the
round table, that are delightful to hear" (Ge sai des romanz d'aventure,/De
cels de la reonde Table,/Qui sont à oïr delitable; ll. 82–84). Pleasant romances, but vain romances; the prologue of a translation into prose of
the *Vies des Pères* (Lives of the Fathers) enjoins: "Leave aside Cligès and
Perceval, that kill hearts and make one feel bad, and all romances of
vanity" (Leissiez Cligés et Perceval/Qui les cuers tue et met a mal/Et les
romanz de vanité; ll. 33–35). Indeed, religious authors often denounce in
one single movement "the fables about Arthur of Brittany and the songs
about Charlemagne" (les fables d'Arthur de Bretaigne/Et les chançons de
Charlemaigne), as is done by Frère Angier in his *Life of Saint Gregory*.

The Arthurian repertory, as with that of the *chansons de geste*, is well
known to its listeners and readers, to such a point that some storytellers,
in a comical vein, have fun playing with the titles of the most famous

works, deforming them and altering their terms. Renart, in the branch of *Renart jongleur* (1b), spoonerizing the names, sings of "Olivant and of Rollier" (Olivant et de Rollier; ll. 2854). More surprisingly, we find the formula at the opening of the *Histoire sainte*, whose incipit is signaled by Arthur Långfors (p. 268):[3] "By these quarrels that are sung, about Rolier and Olivant" (Par ce quareles vont chantant / Et de Rolier et d'Olivant). One of the *deux bordeors ribauz* affirms: "I know how to speak badly of Gawain and of Kay the good knight" (De Gauvain sai le mal parler, / Et de Quex le bon chevalier; ll. 85–86)—the characteristic traits of the two knights have been interchanged, making Gawain the slanderous and Kay the good knight. He continues: "Thus, I know more than forty laisses about Perceval of Blois and about Pertenoble le Gallois" (Si sai de Perceval de Blois; / De Pertenoble le Galois / Sai ge plus de .XL. laisses; ll. 87–89), where the titles have exchanged their terms. We recognize Perceval le Gallois and Partonopeus de Blois.

The list of famous Arthurian characters or heroes of *chansons de geste* is often used to emphasize the valor of a new hero called upon to surpass his predecessors. The author of *Richard le Beau* does not hesitate to begin in this way. The repertoires mentioned are adapted to the intended audience or are copied directly from the personal history of the individual intended to pronounce them. Renart, a supposedly English jongleur, says in his deformed French, which allows him to play with the bawdy register:

Ge fot savoir bon lai breton
Et de Merlin et de Noton,
Del roi Artu et de Tristran,
Del chevrefoil, de saint Brandan   (ll. 2389–2392)

(Me buggering know good Breton lay about Merlin and Noton [the devil], of king Arthur and of Tristan, of honeysuckle, of Saint Brendan)

All of the matters that he lists have to do with Great Britain. The honeysuckle (*chèvrefeuille*) refers to the lay of the same name by Marie de France, Saint Brendan to the travels of this Irish monk, an Anglo-Norman version of which dates back to the beginning of the twelfth century. The authors who introduce new matter take care to situate it in relation to the matters of reference. This is what Gerbert de Montreuil does for the *Ro-*

man de la Violette. He says, "A beautiful and delightful story" (Un conte biel et delitable), and specifies, "It is not about the Round Table, nor king Arthur nor his people" (N'est pas de la Reonde Table,/Dou roi Artu ne de ses gens; ll. 33–35). On the other hand, he inscribes his work in relation to Jean Renart's *Romance of the Rose* and the novelty introduced by Renart of inserting lyrical pieces in a narrative framework. Jean Renart says, "For, if one wants to, one can sing and read it" (car, s'en vieult, l'en i chante et lit; l. 19), Gerbert de Montreuil echoes him, "For one can read and sing it" (Car on i puet lire et chanter; l. 38).

Writing About Troy and Alexander

Referred to as the matter of Rome by Jean Bodel, the romances of Antiquity appear in French in the first third of the twelfth century with a *Roman d'Alexandre* owed to Albéric de Pisançon. The language is Franco-Provençal. Next there is the succession of the three great monuments: the *Roman de Thèbes*, inspired by Statius's *Thebaid*; the *Eneas* (c. 1155), based on Virgil's *Aeneid*; and Benoît de Sainte-Maure's *Roman de Troie* (c. 1165), drawing on two texts purported to be by eyewitnesses of the Trojan War: the *Ephemeri Belli Troiani* by Dictys of Crete (fourth century CE), on the side of the Greeks, and the *De excidio Trojae historia* by Dares Phrygius (sixth century CE), on the Trojan side. This classical subject matter brings together two elements with the promise of a long future together: warfare and love.

In *Flamenca*, a thirteenth-century romance in langue d'oc, more than fifteen hundred jongleurs participate in the wedding of the heroine (l. 504). The romance delivers their repertoire over more than two hundred lines. As regards the classical matter, the text lists Alexander, Troy, Aeneas, and Thebes, to which it adds a mention of the romance of *Apollonius of Tyre* and some allusions to famous couples having provided subject matter for short stories, such as *Pyramus and Thisbe*, and for lays singing of famous heroes, such as Narcissus and Orpheus. The taste for classical matter in the domain of romance and history evolved at the court of Burgundy, where Charles the Bold enjoyed hearing the histories of Alexander, Cyrus, Hannibal, and Caesar being read [in the fifteenth century].

French and English writers alike hazarded polemics drawing their subject matter from France and Brittany, but in each case with reference to classical originals. All the heroes, all the founders invoked on either side, descend from Aeneas. Around 1155, in his *Roman de Brut*, at the request of Henry II Plantagenet, Wace relates the installation of Brutus and of his companions in Great Britain. He follows Geoffroy de Monmouth's *Historia regum Britanniae*, composed some twenty years earlier. *La Petite Philosophie*, an abridged text on cosmography and geography from the beginning of the thirteenth century, which gives the etymology of the different countries' names, says of France: "As for her [France], she is named France from the name of the Frankish king who conquered her, who came from Troy with Aeneas and founded a new Troy on the Rhine" (Elle reest France numee,/Del roi Franc ke l'out cunquesté,/Ke de Troie vint od Enee,/E Troie ad sur le Rhin fundee; ll. 1137–1140). In the same way, at the end of the Middle Ages, the conflicts between France and Burgundy feed on the epic subject matter and on the *gestes* of traitorous barons.

On Love

Returning to England at the end of his life, in 1395, Jean Froissart offered King Richard II a manuscript of all of his poems. He recounts: "The king then asked me what it was about. I said to him: 'about love'" (Adont me demanda le roy de quoy il traittoit. Je luy dis: "D'amours").

Throughout the Middle Ages love is the great subject, for two reasons. One is the poet's: love is the only subject for song. To love is to sing. The other is the audience's. As Christine de Pizan reminds us in the *Cent Ballades*: "The feeling that is the lightest and that pleases everybody the most is love" (Le sentiment qui est le plus legier,/Et qui mieulx plaist a tous de commun cours,/C'est d'amours; Ballade L), or again in the *Epistre Othea*: "And because the matter of love is more pleasant to hear than any other, they made with common accord their fictions about love in order to be more pleasant" (Et pour ce que la matiere d'amours est plus delitable a ouÿr que d'autre, firent communement leurs ficcions sus amours pour estre plus delitables; Histoire 82). In the repertoires of jongleurs that the texts offer, there are the "sounds of love" (*sons d'amours*). It is these that the jongleur sings to the hero of the epic poem *Hervis de Metz* (l. 2476).

Very often this subject matter is broken down into genres. Jean Maillart begins his *Roman du Comte d'Anjou* by listing the subject matters broached by his confreres. He ends up singing about them:

De Robichon et d'Amelot
Li auquant chantent pastourelles;
Li autre dïent en vïelles
Chançons royaus et estempies,
Dances, noctes et baleriez,
En leüst, en paslterion,
Chascun selonc s'entencion,
Lais d'amours, descors et balades,
Pour esbatre ces genz malades   (ll. 11–18)

(About Robichon and Amelot, some sing pastourelles; others play royal songs and estampies, dance tunes, musical pieces and ballets, on hurdy-gurdies, lutes, or psalteries, each according to his inspiration, lays about love, lyrical pieces and ballades, to entertain the sick).

To these entertainments, he opposes that which he himself has chosen to deal with: "a veritable adventure" (l. 38) that must serve as an example. Singing of love goes well beyond simple entertainment. The troubadours and trouvères, up until Guillaume de Machaut, see their literature as being born of love, fueled by love. For them, therefore, love is more than a theme; it is the motive force of their writing. Along with warfare, love is the subject matter of song and of romances. It defines a context specific to medieval writing that has been called courtliness [*courtoisie*], the atmosphere of the courts in which one writes in praise of the ladies. Finally, it is perceived as a totalizing knowledge subsuming all thought, as the *Romance of the Rose* magnificently demonstrates. Love teaches and can be taught. Numerous texts in the Middle Ages are entitled *Arts d'amour* (Arts of love) or assume titles that picturesquely underline the notions of teaching, of didacticism, with regards to love: in *La Clef d'amors* (The Key to Love), for example, the god of Love calls on his author to make him in the form of a "petit portehors," a little book to be carried outside (l. 102), which the lover could always have with him, a book with a practical purpose. The humorous pose is obvious, but it shows the importance attributed to the book in these matters. Ovid's *Ars amatoria* (Art of Love)

is at the origin of these texts, and many such works in French are presented as glossed translations of Ovid. Chrétien de Troyes recalls in the
first lines of his *Cligès* that he has translated the *Ars amatoria*.

But why should texts teach about love, and which love? What is the
link between love and knowledge? All of the terms employed, in fact,
outside of *art*, are those of *treatise*, of *doctrine*, of *science*, of *teaching*.
The great categories of love that are considered are shaped on the object
of love: a woman, one's fellow man, God. As far as the love of women is
concerned, another book, aside from the *Ars amatoria*, had some influence: Andreas Capellanus's *De amore*, dating from the end of the twelfth
century, which Drouart la Vache translated in 1290 under the title *Li
Livres d'amours* (The Book of Love). This is sometimes cited as *De arte
honeste amandi* (The Art of Courtly Love), and the qualifier *honeste*
(honest) is usually translated into modern French as *courtois* (courtly).

How are the arts of love presented? The works that follow [Ovid's]
Ars amatoria most closely are essentially offered as books of manners,
on behavior. They teach the lover to polish his manners, just as the arts
of rhetoric teach one to polish one's words. They give the lover the means
to entrap the lady, and they offer to the lady advice on cheating on her
lover. This is the *ars* in the sense of a ruse, and love is quite homonymous,
in these cases, with the hook (*hameçon*), according to the pair *aim-haim*
(the roots of the words "love" and "hook" in French).

The *Arts* influenced by Andreas Capellanus seek to characterize love,
to give a definition of it, and propose models of conversation. They are
filled with the analysis of its birth and development, often thanks to the
metaphor of the tree. We are looking at a phenomenology. Here again, in
this birth of love, the role of books is essential. Reading books that speak
of love incites one to love. Such is the position of the author of the *Com-
mens d'Amours* (The Beginning of love) attributed to Richard de Fournival by Claude Fauchet in the sixteenth century, and of the anonymous
L'Art d'amours en prose (The Art of Love in Prose): "Such can read and
listen to the art of love who, if he hadn't read it, would never have the
desire nor the will to love" (tel puet lire et oïr l'art d'amours qui s'il ne
l'eüst leü, ja n'eüst talent ne volanté d'amer; ll. 105–106, ed. Bruno Roy,
p. 67).

In the background, we see appear the important question of the innate
and the acquired, of nature and nurture (*nourreture*), according to the

terms of the times. The art of love is not presented solely in the form of didactic treatises. It can be developed in acts by means of the romance or the poem. This is the case of the *Romance of the Rose* "where the art of Love is all enclosed" (ou l'art d'Amors est tote enclose; l. 38). There are numerous works that take up one or another of these teachings or that reuse the actual formula of the *Romance of the Rose*: "ou l'art d'Amors est tote enclose." Reading the *Romance of the Rose* is the advice that Venus gives to the lover in Nicole de Margival's *Dit de la Panthère*: "He who wants to come to understand love will find the science—seed in the other manuscript—contained in the *Romance of the Rose*" (qui veult d'amors a chief venir,/Dedens le Rommant de la Rose/Trouvera la science enclose; ll. 1032–1034). Loyalty recalls this teaching to Heart in the *Livre du Cuer d'amour espris* (The Book of the Love-Smitten Heart) by René of Anjou: "Take the time to read and to see the very beautiful *Romance of the Rose*, where the art of love is enclosed" (Prenez paine a lire et a veoir/Le tresbel Romant de la Rose/La ou l'art d'amours est enclose; ll. 2224–2226). She refers very specifically to the ten commandments of the god Love. Jean Froissart, in his *Joli Buisson de Jonece*, goes back to the formula of his illustrious predecessor to speak of his *Orloge amoureux* (Amorous clock): "Where a great part of the art of Love resides" (Ou grant part del art d'Amours loge; l. 446). Nonetheless, he makes use of a light effect of modesty, by using the nuance: "A large part of the art of Love" (une grande part de l'art d'Amour). Martin le Franc, who analyzes the *Orloge* in his *Trial of Womankind* (*Le Champion des Dames*), places it, by the formulation that he uses, in the realm of Andreas Capellanus: "The amorous clock, where the art of wise love is well presented" (L'orloge amoureux, ou l'art/De sage amour est bien traictié; ll. 12123–12124). The adjective *sage* (wise) echoes the *honeste* of *De arte honeste amandi*. In 1389, Henry Suso's *Horologium Sapientiae* (Clock of Wisdom), written in 1339, was translated into French. The parallelism of the titles through their recourse to an image of technical knowledge, the clock, reveals the tension that organizes the thought of the whole era between love and wisdom.

"The material is of God"

Can God be considered a subject of writing? Is it not the thought of Him that underlies all medieval writing? Recall the formula used by Adam de la Halle: "The material is of God and warfare and love" (Li matere est de Dieu et d'armes et d'amours). God is the constant of this literature. Nevertheless, some authors attach their activity specifically to religious subject matter. Huon le Roi de Cambrai does this when he concludes his *Regres Nostre Dame* (Regrets of Our Lady), saying: "The subject of God is so big that one could talk about him for one hundred years" (La matere est de Dieu si grans/C'om em porroit parler cent ans; stanza 234).

In order to explore the domain as it is thus conceived, we would have to enter into a breakdown of genres—saints's lives, miracles of Our Lady, prayers, sermons—beyond the scope of this study. *Sumite materiam . . .* Pick a subject [says Horace]. On the contrary, the classification of the negative subject matters proposed by moralist authors—that which must not be read—confirms the large fields established by medievals themselves: *chansons de geste*, Arthurian romances, lyricism, most specifically with the genre of the pastorale. It allows us to specify an additional field: the subject matter that evokes laughter, the most often cited example being the *Roman de Renart*.

In his *Life of Sainte Christine,* Gautier de Coincy, one of the most virulent denigrators of entertaining literature, of "romances of vanity," deplores that the audience prefers listening to how "Renart betrays his complice Ysengrin, or a big nonsensical text" (Renart traï Ysengrin son compere,/Ou une grant oiseuse [*oiseuse* means idle but refers as well to a literary genre of nonsense]; ll. 10–11), rather than "an example about either a holy man or a holy woman or a good text" (de saint ne de sainte essample ne bon dit). Nevertheless, he shows in this that he is familiar with this repertoire. He cites with precision different branches of the animal *geste* and some of its characters: Romer (a variant of the name of the ass, ordinarily called Bernard), Tardif the snail, Coupée the hen. The large divide in Gautier de Coincy's mind occurs between vanity and truth, between laughter and teaching, even though he knows well, and says in the prologue to his second book of *Miracles,* that what pleases the audience are "long fables and short sermons" (longues fables et sermons courts; l. 149). In this prologue, he affirms his poetic art loud and clear in a litany of binary formulae, admirably tough: "I want to follow the prophet rather than the poet" (Plus veil enssivre le prophète/Que je ne face le poete; ll. 65–66). Between the literature inspired by the Holy Spirit and the pagan authors, he chooses Saint John and Saint Luke over Lucan; the Gospel over Juvenal and Virgil. In a word, he says, better the fruit than the leaf.

Gautier de Coincy, being a great writer, makes wise use of another advantage religious matter presents; it is unlimited. The author does not have to worry about his worst fear: "the lack of material" (la defaillance de matere; l. 53 of the first prologue of the first collection). Gautier arrives at a logical consequence, as proof for those he needs to convince of the superiority of this matter: there is no need to invent, "to find lies," "Mary is a sea that nobody can exhaust" (Marie est mer que nus espuise; l. 49).[4]

In the fourteenth century, Jean Le Fèvre also proceeds by means of a negative definition of the literary field. He opens his *Respit de la Mort* declaring "I do not want to deal with love" (je ne voeil par traitier d'amours), a refusal of lyrical matter; "nor with warfare" (ne d'armez), a refusal of the epic matter; "nor do I want to make noise about Fortune or her wheel" (ne faire clamours/De Fortune ne de sa roe), a refusal of the moral subjects addressed in an allegorical manner. In the same way, he repudiates Renart and Louvel, the wolf, in other words, the subject matter of Renart. He does this to the benefit of a different subject: death. In the twelfth century already, Hélinand of Froidmont had opposed, in his *Vers de la Mort*, "Those who sing of love and who brag of vanity" (Caus qui d'amours chantent/Et qui de vanité se vantent) to those who sing of death (stanza 2). Jean Le Fèvre, though not in Hélinand's form of an incantatory lyrical text, but in that of a *dit*, pursues this personal vein. He starts with a reflection on his own death, death that brushed up against him and from which he wants to obtain a *répit* (respite) to address, by means of a non sequitur (*coq à l'asne*), various moral and philosophical subjects. But not until Montaigne will an author use a formula this new right at the outset, expressed in precisely these terms: "And so, reader, I am myself the matter of my book" (Ainsi, lecteur, je suis moy-mesmes la matiere de mon livre).

CHAPTER SIX

The Paths to Writing

Assembling his "complete works," an entirely new practice at the time, Guillaume de Machaut precedes them with a theoretical reflection, a mirror *en abyme* of the entirety of the work: four ballades and a commentary in octosyllables. He evokes the forces that are at the origin of his writing: Nature and Love. Nature provides form to his poetry in the gift of three children: Sense, Rhetoric, and Music. Love supplies him with the subject matter through a parallel gift of three other children: Sweet Thought, Pleasure, and Hope. As this arrangement shows, the form comes first.

The same applies to the domain of divine creation. Is God not "He who formed, without matter, the world and the whole human lineage" (Celli qui forma sans matiere / Le monde et tout l'umain lignage), as asserted by *The Legend of Saint John Damascene* in the *Tombel de Chartrose* (ll. 674–675)?

The form also comes first in the literary domain. It governs the composition through Sense. The key word, in fact, is that of order, of organization, referring us back to the notion of harmony. Moreover, for Guillaume de Machaut, as for Dante, Rhetoric and Music play a prominent role. Let us remember the definition of poetry proposed by Dante in the *De vulgari eloquentia*: "a verbal invention composed according to the rules of rhetoric and music" (fictio rethorica musicaque poita; 2.4.4).

The pair, matter and form, can be reworked into adjacent binomials. One is created by the rhyme: matter and manner. But the concept of form is also expressed with words such as *façon* (way), *contenant* (that which contains), or *contenance* (manner) that designate from the outset the general aspect or the appearance of a being or of a person, or more specifically a person's face. But these terms also offer metadiscursive uses for referring to the form of a work or, to be more precise, its style. Martin le Franc, speaking of Guillaume Dufay and Binchois, two musicians of his time, praises them in his *Champion des Dames* (Trial of Womankind), saying: they "have adopted the English manner" (ont prins de la contenance/Angloise; ll. 16269–16270). The word *style* came into use at the end of the Middle Ages, signaling the awareness of the mark the subject makes on a work, the insertion of a personality. In *L'Advision Cristine*, Christine de Pizan rejoices in having found through study what she calls: "my natural style" (le stille a moy naturel; 3.10, p. 110). Dante similarly congratulates himself on having acquired *lo bello stilo* (the noble style) through reading Virgil (*Inferno* 1.87).

Beauty

What indeed are the principles that command esthetic judgment? According to Thomas Aquinas's definition of beauty, there are three: *integritas* (completeness, totality, purity); *proportio, consonantia* (proportion, harmony); and *claritas* (clarity, radiance).

Proportio. First of all, order. Measure is a principal that is both moral and esthetic. Art must be measured in order to be beautiful. Thus, even Christine de Pizan's Chaos, who appears at the opening of *L'Advision Cristine*, is beautiful. He has "the stature of a man of beautiful form" (l'estature d'un homme de belle forme; p. 12) and Christine specifies: "In this statue there was nothing deformed" (En ceste statue n'avoit riens de difforme). Only his extreme pain shows him as a being from disorder. This shows the power of the criterion of harmony, which functions even when dealing with the horrifying.

La Vision de Tondale, in the French translation of Vincent de Beauvais' Latin, displays the same reticence about disproportion. In its evocation of the horrible, the French text in fact introduces a respect for the notion of relative measure that is not in the Latin text, saying of Lucifer: "He also had a very long tail suited to his body in thickness and in length" (Il avoit aussi une moult grant queue a l'avenant de son corps en grosseur et en longueur), and: "He had an iron beak very long and wide, just as his body needed to have" (Il avoit ung becq de fer moult long et moult gros selonc ce que son corps requeroit avoir).

Literary texts sometimes assert the need to respect proportions in the construction of a work. The author of the *Suite du Roman de Merlin* indicates, for example:

It is suitable that the three parts of my book be equal, each as long as the others. And if I were to add this long story [meaning the story of *Lancelot*], the middle part of my book would be three times longer than the other two. For this reason I must leave out this great story that traces the deeds of Lancelot and his birth.

(Il convient que les .III. parties de mon livre soient ingaus, l'une aussi grant coume l'autre. Et se je ajoustaisse cele grant ystore, la moienne partie de mon livre fust au tresble plus grand que les autres deus. Pour chou me couvient il laissier celle grant ystorie qui devise les oevres de Lanscelot et la naissance; § 239)

Others specify, at times obsessively, that their books call for formal construction. The anonymous author of the *Trésor amoureux* in the fourteenth century has such a protocol presented by the god Love, who even teaches him how to compile a table of the lyrical pieces that have been inserted. The author goes back to these indications in the third stanza of the first ballade. The didacticism in matters of poetic composition is mixed in with the teachings about love. Significantly, the refrain of this ballade adds a third term to the canonical pair of warfare and love found in chivalrous poetry. The poet intends to speak, "Of warfare, of love and of morality" (D'armes, d'amours et de moralité; p. 77).

To be harmonious, the work must be constructed as a whole. For many authors, there is the feeling of an organic composition attached to a work such that it must not be dismembered or taken apart. This is what Jaufré Rudel teaches in his song "He who does not write a melody does not know how to sing" (No sap chantar qui so non di). One must not break (*franbar*), nor take apart (*pessiar*) the song (l. 34). In *Erec et Enide*, Chrétien de Troyes criticizes venal storytellers for this breaking into pieces: "Those who try to live by storytelling customarily mangle and corrupt" (Depecier et corrompre suelent/Cil qui de conter vivre vuelent; ll. 21–22), extolling the *mout bele conjunture* (beautifully ordered composition; l. 14) that he has imposed on the subject matter he received.

The word *conjointure* is rare in Old French, and it no doubt derives from clerical terminology. We do not encounter it before Chrétien de Troyes. It is present in the work of Everat (Evrat), translator of the Book of Genesis into French verse for Marie de Champagne, who was also the recipient of Chrétien's *Knight of the Cart*. Everat uses *conjointure* to refer to the soul, thanks to which God changes an amorphous form into an organic whole. In his *Chronique rimée* (Rhymed Chronicle), Philippe Mousket applies the term to a portrait of Grammar painted, along with the other liberal arts, on the walls of Charlemagne's palace: "First was painted Grammar, who teaches us in what way we must write figures and assemble *conjointures*" (Gramare i fu painte première / Qui nos ensegne en quel manière / On doit escrire les figures / Et asambler les congointures; ll. 9702–9705).

We must read a moral and religious principle behind this ideal of a composed unity, it seems. In the same way that God is both three and one, the work must join together its parts—there are often three of them—into one whole. The principle is simultaneously advocated by classical rhetoric and religious thought.

A whole without seams, such is Christ's tunic that the guards argue over. They gamble for it with dice, they tear it apart, destroying what was perfect, bringing multiplicity to what was unity. The devil is the great divider, as indicated by his name [in Greek *diabolos,* cognate with] *diabolē* (that which separates). Therefore the supreme skill, for the mechanical arts, is to imitate divine perfection, to build objects of which we cannot see the *jointures* (seams). This is the marvel that magic creates when it manages to rival nature, to imitate the work of God. Jean, the skilled architect in Chrétien de Troyes' romance *Cligès*, has constructed a tower whose underground passages shelter the supposedly dead Fenice behind a door in which "never will you find a crack" (ja n'i troverez jointure; l. 5514). The fairy Esclarmonde in Girart d'Amiens' *Escanor* builds a fountain in such a way, "That it would seem to you visibly to have no seams, the work being of such a great nature" (Qu'il vouz semblast visablement / Que nuz n'y coneüst jointure, / Tant fu l'uevre de grant nature; ll. 16062–16064).

What about literary works? There is an esthetic of the *round* work, this is the vocabulary used by the texts, which, like a crown, can nevertheless be composed of various pieces arranged into a perfect shape.

This goes both for the work and for the collection. Eustache Deschamps speaks in this way of a volume of his works that has been borrowed from him and not returned:

Poeterie fut au tour du sercel
Rhetorique le fist ront comme annel.   (BALLADE 984, 5: 229)

(*Art poétique* was a part of this circle, Rhetoric made it round like a ring.)

The author of the *Mesnagier de Paris* (The Householder of Paris) is exemplary when it comes to the double impulse that pushes one to compose by adding text, on the one hand and, on the other hand, to preserve the integrity of the work that is being inserted. Inserting into his own text the work of another author, *La Voie de Povreté et de Richesse* (The Way of Poverty or Riches) by Jacques Bruyant, he comments: "And for this reason, I do not want to gut [or, perhaps, mutilate] his book, nor to take out of it one single chip nor separate it from the rest" (Et pour ce ne vueil je mie son livre estrippeller, ne n'en oser un coippel ne le departir du remenant; p. 412). The book in its entirety serves, therefore, as an argument for the author of the *Mesnagier* in his demonstration. He justifies himself in the same way for having inserted the entire story of Sarah, although only one point—Sarah obeying her husband—is relevant to his subject. He explains, "And I did not wish to dismember nor separate it because the matter is beautiful and holds itself together" (Et ne l'ay voulu desmembrer ne descoupler pour ce que la matiere est belle et s'entretient; p. 166). The Middle Ages combine, then, an esthetic of the whole with an esthetic of formal discontinuity. Only a strong feeling of unity allows the caesura.

Integritas, consonantia, claritas. The third esthetic precept, clarity, is magnificently illustrated in the domain of architecture by Suger. Beauty is light, a light that transfigures the matter, making it intelligible—gothic architecture bears witness to this. In the fourteenth century, in her *Dit de Poissy*, Christine de Pizan exalts the beauty of the church of the abbey of Poissy in these terms: "it is so beautiful, high, clear" (tant est bel, hault, cler; l. 470).

How can the esthetic of light be captured in a literary work? Texts work at it, describing scenes around radiant objects—the Grail, in particular—by evoking the luminous objects or countrysides, by exalting the glowing beauty of women: their skin color, their eyes, their smile. Authors seek to "illuminate" their works, not only in the technical sense, with miniatures that can accompany them, but also with the beauty of their very words. The author of *Richard le Beau* claims to rhyme a "very well composed adventure" that he "illuminates" with "many beautiful words" (aventure mout bien ditée; enlumine; mout biaus dis; ll. 71–74). Charles of Orléans depicts his heart writing in his book of thought "the true story of pain, of tears, all illuminated" (la vraye histoire de douleur/De larmes toute enluminée; rondeau 107). Guillaume de Machaut affirms in his "Prologue": "And if one composes on a sad subject, joyous is the manner of doing it" (Et s'on fait de triste matiere/Si est joieuse la maniere/Dou fait; ll. 43–45). The light that can also be viewed in the moral domain as truth is a part of the joy that presided at the creation. It gives a soul and a sense to the matter.

The Pleasant

In addition to the esthetic principals that can be defined in the works are principles of pleasure that are regularly invoked. First of all, novelty. The proverb says it, and the medieval authors repeat it: "All that is new pleases" (Tout plaist quanqui est nouvel).

This taste for novelty is even attributed to Nature who renews herself each spring. The author of *Renart le Contrefait* insists: "Nature rejoices to the highest degree when she listens to a new story. Nature has fun looking for new people and new land" (Nature s'i s'esjoïst toute,/Quant nouvelle histoire elle escoute:/Nouvelles gens, nouvelle terre,/Nature s'esbat a l'enquerre; ll. 3245–3248). Here he is justifying his literary undertaking by invoking this philosophical model: "This is the reason that I want to renew this *Roman de Renart*" (Pour ce voeul je nouvellement/De Regnard faire ce rommant; ll. 3249–3250).

But in the same way that, at times, pleasure might go against moral benefit, the search for novelty can enter into conflict with the values linked to that which is old. This tension leads to deeper reflection on the term "newness," to which medieval people attribute two meanings: the "new" in the sense of that which is full of freshness and can, therefore, be a renewal—new grass, a new rose in love poetry—and the "new" as in that which has never been seen before.

The positive new, the renewal, does not go against the old: it reju-
venates it, regenerates it. Thus, in the thirteenth century, Herbert, the
author of the *Roman de Dolopathos*, says to be putting his Latin source
into French because "The story is good and beautiful, it should always be
new, for a thing from which good can be born shall never grow old" (Li
estore est et bonne et belle,/toz jors dovroit estre novelle,/car jai vielz ne
doit devenir/choze dont bien peut avenir; ll. 15–18). He seems to propose
a defense of modernization by means of translation.

On the other hand, the negative meaning of "new" brings about
clashes with moral values and criticism on the part of religious authors.
The author of the *Tombel de Chartrose*, in his thirteenth tale, assimilates
"novelties" with "lies and fables" and opposes them to the "good, holy
and profitable words of the old institutions" (bons sains motz prouf-
fitables/Des viulles institucions; ed. Kooiman, p. 102).

But this aspect of the new brings about, from an esthetic point of view,
an emphasis placed on a particular qualifier that then takes on positive
values: the strange. Guillaume de Machaut, in his *Voir-dit* speaks of the
song that he wrote based on his ballade of which the refrain is, "The great
desire that I have to see you" (Le grant desir que j'ai de vous veoir). He
comments: "I wrote the song from *Le grant desir que j'ai de vous veoir*,
just as you asked me to. And I wrote it in the German style. And truly it
seems to me very strange and very new" (J'ay fait le chant sur *Le grant
desir que j'ai de vous veoir*, ainsi comme vous le m'avez commandé. Et
l'ai fait ainsi comme un rés d'Alemaigne. Et vraiment il me semble moult
estranges et moult nouviaus; letter 4, p. 128). There is a pleasure in the
renewed. The melody has a model, but the new composition creates the
particular beauty that is designated by the term "strange."

A series of ambivalent terms is to be considered. Diverse. The morally
diverse is to be blamed. This goes, for example, for the *fame diverse*, the
bad reputation of Béthisac, the duc de Berry's treasurer in Languedoc,
in Froissart's work (*Chronicles*, book 4, ed. A. Varvaro, p. 404). On the
other hand, esthetically speaking, diversity can be a criterion for beauty.
It contributes to what the author of the *Tombel de Chartrose* calls the
"pleasure of novelty" (*plaisance de nouveauté*).

Opinions on the new ways of singing clashed too: on the hocket, for
example, that works with the broken line. The French term for hocket,
hoquet, also means to hiccup. Guillaume de Saint Pathus plays with this

double meaning when he reports in his *Vie de Saint Louis*: "He does not sing the songs of the world. . . . Their songs are hiccoughings, more like mockeries" (Il ne chantoit pas les chançons du monde. . . . Leurs chansons sont hoqueteries, trop mieux ressemblant moquerie). In his decretal *Docta sanctorum* (between 1322 and 1324), Pope John XXII, for his part, very strongly criticizes the innovations of the *Ars nova* (new art). This opposition, on the beauty or not of calculated dismemberment, runs through all of the arts: music as well as fashion or literature.

An Awareness of Forms

VERSE AND PROSE

Verse comes first in literary writing; verse is first in that it is linked to singing. Different measures are found in it, measures that give rhythm and distinguish genres: the narrative octosyllable, the epic decasyllable that is eventually replaced by the monumental alexandrine. The latter, in fact, is the verse of funerary inscriptions in late medieval texts, in René of Anjou's cemetery in particular. The heptasyllable is found sporadically in texts that seek to be marginal. Such is the case for *Aucassin et Nicolette*, a unique representative of the genre that the text refers to with the term *chantefable* (song-tale). It mixes parts that are sung in heptasyllabic *laisses* ending with a short (four-syllable) line with parts that are spoken, according to the scansion: "now it is sung," "now spoken and told and made up" (or se chante; or dient et content et fabloient).

Prose, at its earliest occurrence in literary texts, first appears in translations of the Bible: a translation of the *Quatre Livres des Rois* (middle of the twelfth century), about which it is debated whether it is rhymed prose or a poem in prose. In any case, prose goes on to become the great form, not only of romances in the thirteenth century, for example, *The High History of the Holy Grail* (known also by the name of *Perlesvaus*), the Prose *Lancelot*, and the Prose *Tristan*, but also of historical matter coming from witnesses: *The Conquest of Constantinople*, by Geoffrey of Villehardouin and Robert de Clari, and *Vie de saint Louis* (Life of Louis IX), by Joinville.

Prose in the Middle Ages, for both positive and negative reasons, is linked to the idea of truth. By the way it presents itself, the *Haut Livre du Graal* plays an important role in this link between prose and the true word. A continuation of Chrétien de Troyes' *Conte du Graal* (Story of the Grail), it is presented as having been dictated by an angel who transmitted the revelations of the Holy Ghost. The angel spoke Latin, of course, but the book is represented as nothing other than the work of God, "From God comes the high story of the Grail" (de Dieu, si muet li hauz contes du Graal). This gives us a positive link between prose and the word of God.

The negative reason proceeds from a contrast with verse, which is accused of being forced to lie by the constraints of the rhyme. Pierre de Beauvais, in his *Bestiary*, justifies his choice of prose by accusing lines of verse of "being adorned with words picked from outside of the truth" (s'afaitier de moz concueilliz hors de verité). The prologue of the *Pseudo Turpin Chronicle* contains an analogous formula for repudiating rhyme that "wants to be adorned with words gathered outside of history" (se velt afeitier de moz conqueilliz hors de l'estoire). For this reason, the book will be "without rhyme, following the story in Latin that Turpin, the archbishop of Reims, dealt with and wrote according to what he saw and heard" (sanz rime selonc le latin de l'estoire que Torpins l'arcevesque de Reins traita et escrist si com il le vit et oï). Yet, as we know, the author of the text is fictitious, making the proclamation of truth all the stronger. Still at the end of the Middle Ages, in his prose version of *La Belle Hélène de Constantinople*, Jean Wauquelin says that he wants to "cut out and omit the useless prolongations and words that often are used and aligned in such rhymes" (retranchier et sincoper les prolongations et mots inutiles qui souvent sont mis et boutez en telles rimes).

For the authors who write both prose and verse, the choice is a question of taste, at times expressed even in culinary terms. Richard de Fournival, who wrote his *Bestiary of Love* in prose, offers a version of it in verse with this justification: "So that we have a little, some roasted some boiled. May each choose what he wishes and that which will please him the most to listen to" (Por ce que on en ait un peu,/Puis en rost et puis en esceu; Si praingn'on le quel c'on vaurra/Et qui a oïr miex plaira). An accurate comparison of the two forms, which both fall under the category of art, can be found in the *Trésor* by Brunetto Latini. He writes in his third part, dedicated to rhetoric:

> But the teachings of rhetoric are common to both forms, except that the way to prose is large and ample, as is today the usual way that

people speak, while the way to rhyme is enclosed and surrounded with walls and palisades, that is to say of weight and number and a certain measure.

(Mais li ensegnement de rectorique sont commun d'ambes .II., sauve ce que la voie de prose est large et pleniere, si comme est ore la commune parleure des gens, mais li sentiers de risme est plus estrois et plus fors, si comme celui ki est clos et fermés de murs et de palis, c'est a dire de pois et de nombre et de mesure certaine; 3.10)

We read in the apocryphal gospels (*Wisdom* 11:21) that God balanced the world in measure, number, and weight. We recognize this formula in Brunetto Latini. In medieval thought, the number is in God, the number is God. At the beginning of the thirteenth century, Henry of Avranches devotes himself to showing the analogy that exists between God and poetry. We are far from Boileau who writes in his *Satires*: "Cursed be the first whose foolish inspiration, in the confines of a line of verse enclosed his thought and, giving to his words a narrow prison, wanted to enslave reason with rhyme" (Maudit soit le premier dont la verve insensée/Dans les bornes d'un vers renferma sa pensée,/Et donnant à ses mots une étroite prison,/Voulut avec la rime enchaîner la raison). Verse is not a prison for the Middle Ages, not any more than prose is without measure. Both belong to an order, the order of the world, the order of God.

RHYME AND REASON

All combinations are possible, verse with verse, verse with prose. A technique is developed starting in the thirteenth century that grafts stanzas of lyrical poetry into texts of narrative verse according to an esthetic of ornamental quotation. Jean Renart's *Romance of the Rose*—called *Guillaume de Dole*, the name of its hero, by Claude Fauchet, in the sixteenth century, and later critics, in order to distinguish it from Guillaume de Lorris and Jean de Meun's *Romance of the Rose*, offers one of the first examples of this conjunction:

Car aussi com l'en met la graine
Es dras por avoir los et pris,
Einsi a il chans et son mis

En cestui Romans de la Rose
Qui est une novele chose
Et s'est des autres si divers
Et brodez, par lieus de biaux vers
Que vilains nel porroit savoir   (ll. 8–15)

(For as one soaks clothing with red dye so that they are admired and coveted, in such a way he has inserted songs and their melody in this *Romance of the Rose*. This is a new thing, so different from the others, so well embroidered, beautiful verse here and there, that a boor would not know how to appreciate it.)

Novelty and diversity: these are indeed the esthetic criteria identified here. This esthetic that we call "collage" can give up its place in other cases to an esthetic of assemblage that consists of building a story through the narration of lyrical pieces that have been inserted. Guillaume de Machaut accomplishes this in his *Dits*, in the *Voir-dit* in particular.

The texts call for verse and prose according to very diverse patterns: an alternation like in *Aucassin et Nicolette* or a succession as we find in Rutebeuf's *Dit de l'Herberie*.

Other patterns are possible. A text in verse may receive a commentary in prose: this is the case in the *Epître Othea* by Christine de Pizan; a story in prose, in the manner of the prose texts of the (Holy) Grail, may insert characters' lines in verse; as in René of Anjou's *Coeur d'Amours espris* (Love-Smitten Heart).

Finally, the combinations of verse and prose in the works of the Grands Rhétoriqueurs explore all of the possibilities of confrontation. The great scholarly model is Boethius's *De consolatione philosophiae* [*The Consolation of Philosophy*; early sixth century CE].

MODELS OF STANZAS AND THEIR USE

For a narration, the most common form of versification is the octosyllabic couplet. But a few types of stanzaic groups were especially popular, and some of them formally define genres or subgenres that distinguish their theme. In this way, the *laisse* is the unity of composition for the epic poem.

A substantive taken from the verb *laissier* (to leave), the word *laisse* refers to a grouping of lines of verse for which the only constraint is the identity of the final assonance, or, in a more recent time, the identity of the rhyme. Of variable length, the *laisses* in the *chansons de geste* go from four lines for the shortest of them in the *Charroi de Nîmes* to 191 lines for the longest *laisse* in the *Moniage Guillaume*. They are chanted, and signaled by a specific tone for the introduction and another specific tone for the conclusion.

The decasyllable is the meter of the early *chanson de geste*. But after the appearance around 1140 of the parodic *Le Pèlerinage de Charlemagne* (Charlemagne's Pilgrimage) in assonanced alexandrines, this meter became very frequent in this genre in the thirteenth century. Even rewritings of decasyllabic *chansons de geste* in alexandrines—*Jourdain de Blaye*, for example— are found as early as the thirteenth century, and especially in the fourteenth and fifteenth centuries.

The form favored in moral literature is the quatrain of monorhymed alexandrines. Significantly, in Rutebeuf's *Miracle de Theophilus*, where the use of versification is so planned, it is in such quatrains that Théophile pronounces his *repentance*, before imploring the Virgin to recover his soul, which he has sold to the devil (ll. 384–431). Rutebeuf uses this form as well for religious satires, such as the criticism of the Order of Preachers in the *Dit des Jacobins*. He uses it for political pieces with the *Dit de Pouille*, written in favor of Charles of Anjou, brother of Saint Louis, and in the *Dit de la voie de Tunes* (Dit of the Tunis Crusade). Jean de Meun uses this metric unit to build his *Testament*, in which he regrets his past literary activity, having in his youth composed "many poems out of vanity" (maint dit par vanité). In the first half of the fourteenth century, the twenty-two *dits* by Jehan de Saint-Quentin are written in this strophic and metric form. As for their themes, there are miracles of the Virgin; folkloric tales with a moral goal, such as the *Dit de Merlin Mellot*; and what the Middle Ages called examples: short stories from which the author draws a moral.

The so-called helinandian stanza, twelve octosyllables with a rhyme scheme of aab aab bba bba, creating a circular pattern, had a specific function: this is the form of all of the leave-takings (*congés)* of the thirteenth century, farewells to the city and to friends, farewell from Jean Bodel, from Baude Fastoul, from Adam de la Halle. The form derives its name from its use by Hélinand of Froidmont in his *Vers de la mort* (Verses of Death).

Rutebeuf's respective use of the two types of forms: quatrains of monorhymed alexandrines and helinandian stanzas is very enlightening. *Le Miracle de Théophile*, in which the cleric of that name repents, is written in quatrains of monorhymed alexandrines, while the piece entitled by some manuscripts *Repentance Rutebeuf* is written in helinandian stanzas. It is as if by changing the metric form, Rutebeuf was formally distinguishing the character Théophile from his persona: Rutebeuf.

What is more, another manuscript calls this piece *La Mort Rutebeuf* (The Death of Rutebeuf). Here, the chosen title places emphasis on the tone induced by the metrics. The stanza brings this piece, which speaks not of death but of repenting, closer to Helinand's *Vers de la mort*.

Two important texts by the Reclus de Molliens, the *Roman de Carité* and *Miserere*, which also look at the question of repentance, are written with this stanzaic form, which was transformed in the fifteenth century by Guillaume Alexis. In his *Blason de faulses amours*, the monk of Lire keeps the mirrored rhyme scheme but breaks away from the unity of the lines. The first eight lines are of four syllables each, the final four lines are of eight, creating a different type of symmetry. This is the metrical pattern that Jean de la Fontaine uses in his tale *Janot et Catin*. He even specifies its medieval origins, but without really knowing the name of the author: "I composed these stanzas in an old style, in the way of the *Blason des fausses amours*" (J'ai composé ces stances en vieil style, à la manière du Blason des fausses amours).

This awareness of forms also shows up in a didactic manner in treatises of poetics or of versification that we find as early as the thirteenth century in the south: *Razos de trobar* by Raimon Vidal, *Regles de trobar* by Jofre de Foixà, who continues them—both authors are Catalan—and *Leys d'Amors* from the Toulousain Consistory of the Gay Science, le *Gai Saber*, at the beginning of the fourteenth century. Poetry is equal to love. It finds its active principle in joy as a condition of the art of composing. Joy is to agree with poetry.

In langue d'oïl, Eustache Deschamps' treatise *L'Art de Dictier* (The Art of Composing), dated November 25, 1392, assumes a particular importance. Deschamps defines what we call poetry as "natural music": "a music of the mouth uttering metered speech" (musique de bouche en proferant paroules metrifiées). Of course, he still categorizes poetry as music and not rhetoric, but he proclaims its autonomous existence, without the support of "artificial music," in other words, the music of instruments.

Eustache Deschamps takes note of an essential mutation in lyricism. In fact, this possible separation from singing, from "the singable voice," gives birth to the modern definition of lyricism as an expression of the self. But the link between natural music—poetry—and the measured voice remains essential to Deschamps. And the ideal remains the union of natural music with artificial music: "a marriage in conjunction with science," he says, where the "songs" are "ennobled" by speech and the "natural songs" are "beautified with melody" (chans; anobliz; chançons natureles; embellies par la melodie).

After this theoretical setting up of poetry, Deschamps engages in a practical analysis: a study of letters and the sounds that they designate, an examination of the models of the principal lyrical forms: ballades, virelays, rondeaux, lays. It is essentially to this technical aspect that the *Arts de seconde rhétorique* (Arts of Second Rhetoric) in the fifteenth century return. The second rhetoric here refers to the art of verse compared to that of prose, the first rhetoric. These treatises propose models of forms, reflections on meters and their privileged uses, and lists both of rhymes and of mythological characters. *Poétrie* in the Middle Ages refers first of all to mythology.

The *Leys d'Amors* give the following definition for the art of composing: "courtly composition consists of making a new poem, in the pure vernacular and well 'compassed' [shaped]" (Trobar es far noel dictat/En romans fi, ben compassat). Such is truly the very essence of *trobar*, the art of writing, in the Middle Ages. There is a need for refined language, pure (*fi*), vernacular (oc or oïl); measured language (*ben compassat*), constructed with a precision that allows for the *noel*, the new.

A SOCIAL VIEW OF FORMS

In the Middle Ages, there was a social view of forms, from the smallest units—rhymes and meters—to the largest, which spectacularly translates the vocabulary of the treatises of rhetoric. These treatises, in their terminology, oppose *rural* and *royal*. The same opposition is made for rhymes. Jean Molinet, in his *Art de rhétorique*, distinguishes poor rhyme and rich rhyme in this way. He qualifies poor rhyme as being *rime en goret* (pig rhyme), when it only concerns one letter, and opposes it to rich rhyme, Leonine rhyme, the equivocal rhyme. The humble pig is the opposite of the king of the animals, the lion, and Molinet specifies, "let the shepherds use their rural rhetoric" (laisse les bergiers user de leur rethorique rurale; p. 249).

In the same way, the treatises mock "the boors and oafs who rhyme beans with nuts" (les ruraulx et lourdois/qui riment feves contre pois), that is to say who confuse a semic relatedness with a phonetic resemblance. Such is the formulation of the *Infortuné* (the wretch) in the *Instructif de la seconde rhétorique*.

One observes a similar type of qualification for some forms or some social groups that produce poetry. Defining the *chant royal,* Molinet says that it "is recited at the poetic contest where crowns and wreaths are given to those who know best how to do it" (chant royal se recorde es puis ou se donnent couronnes et chappeaux a ceulx qui mieulx le scevent faire; ed. Langlois, p. 242); and the *Art et science de rhétorique* says, "chants royaux . . . are recited in the royal poetic contest, where crowns, decorations and laurel wreaths are given to those who know how to do them best and who win the prize" (Chantz royaulx . . . se recordent es puys royaulx, ou se donnent couronnes, palmes et chappeaux de laurier a ceulx qui sçavent mieulx faire et emportent le pris; ed. Langlois, p. 302). Royal, then, does not refer directly to a social place, the king's court, but signals a mastery that gives powers of domination and exclusion to language and rhetoric. The exclusion of the *berger* (shepherd) from these bourgeois fraternities can be turned around into a praise of simplicity that is found in the criticism of courtly life. It is in praise of *Franc Gontier* and of his rustic life that Philippe de Vitry, an important bishop, writes. Yet, as François Villon underlines in his *Contredits Franc Gontier,* only someone who lives a life of ease can have these regrets. Rhetorical simplicity and praise of life in the fields are dreams of powerful people.

Finally, there exists a perception of registers in the use of meters. The alexandrine, through its link with the prestigious emperor, through its length, is felt as more solemn than the octosyllable, and authors use it as a means of social characterization. Jean Malkaraume, in his versified translation of the Bible, leaves aside the octosyllable when celebrating David's lineage. He justifies himself: "Listen therefore to what I will say to you, for I wish to change my verse, as is appropriate when singing of kings" (Or escoutés que je dirai,/Car ma rime muër voudrai,/Com apartient chanter de roi; ll. 8115–8117). He switches to the alexandrine and, using the epic technique, repeats: "I have changed my rhyme, that is just and reasonable for this is a royal song" (J'ai ma rime muee, il est drois et raison,/Je la dois bien müer, car c'est roiaus chanson; ll. 8123–8124). Conversely, all of René of Anjou's epitaphs of important figures in the *Livre du Cuer d'Amours espris* (Book of the Love-Smitten Heart) are in alexandrines, except the one for his servant Louis de Beauvau, which is in octosyllables. Evrart de Conty, in his *Livre des eschez amoureux moralisés* (Book of the Moralized Chess of Love), comments on the social and esthetic value of the alexandrine: "these are such rhymes appropriate for reciting notable stories and marvelous feats of the ancients, for such high matters should be expressed by such measure" (ce sont telles rimes convenables a reciter les histoires notables et les merveilleux fais des anciens, car telles haultes materes se veulent exprimer par telle mesure; p. 169). In the sixteenth century, George Gascoigne explicitly links the chant royal and the royal rhyme in English versification, with the serious style. This social view of rhetoric was common to France and to England.

The Imaginary Realm of Writing

"God is an infinite sphere whose center is everywhere, and the circumference nowhere" (Deus est sphaera infinita cuius centrum est ubique, circumferentia vero nusquam), an anonymous Latin treatise from the second half of the twelfth century entitled *Liber XXIV philosophorum* asserts. Following this formula in his essay "La esfera de Pascal" ("Pascal's Sphere"; 1952), Jorge Luis Borges concludes: "Perhaps universal history is the history of the diverse intonation of a few metaphors" (Quizá la historia universal es la historia de la diversa entonación de algunas metáforas). Metaphorical space, in fact, functions like a great memory, and it can be explored in order to define the concept of writing that medieval authors established for themselves. Writing is a work on form according to two broad categories of models: natural and artificial.

The agricultural metaphor is very widely used and tells of the development, the growth, generally speaking, of man or of one of his virtues, his inscription in time. Here again the general prologue of the *Lais* by Marie de France is eloquent: "When a truly beneficial thing is heard by many people, it then enjoys its first blossom, but if it is widely praised its flowers are in full bloom" (Quant uns granz biens est mult oïz,/Dunc a primes est il fluriz,/E quant loëz est de plusurs,/Dunc ad espandues ses flurs; ll. 5–8—p. 41 of the Burgess and Busby translation).

When applied to writing, this metaphor defines the different moments of the act: seeds, labor, harvesting, gleaning. According to the inflection placed on one or the other of these activities, we notice phases of French literary history: an optimistic phase where the metaphor used is that of seeds—as in Chrétien de Troyes—and a more melancholic phase where the activity of writing defines itself as a gleaning, as is frequently the case in the fourteenth century. However, as early as the twelfth century, some monastic authors writing in Latin, notably St. Bernard, had defined their position with regard to the Fathers of the Church in this way. The delay in the passage of the phenomena from Latin to French is characteristic.

Medieval French writers in some places also call attention to agricultural improvements—in hoeing, pruning, and especially grafting—that are applicable to writing, for which agriculture is a metaphor. Authors like Christine de Pizan and Martin le Franc praise not only the goddess Ceres, who found the art of planting, but also Isis, who developed the art of grafting and is said to have invented writing as well. The result of the composition process, the book, is described in plant terminology. We can distinguish the root, the stem, the flower or, perhaps, the stump, the trunk, the leaf.

Finally, the metaphor can be topographical. The book is thought of as a garden or an orchard. Gautier de Coincy, who mixes songs in honor of the Virgin with his narratives of miracles, says that he wishes in this way to "plant" in his book "Here and there new songs" (De lius en lius chançons noveles), to "strew and embellish it with sweet-smelling flowers" (joncier/Et florir d'odorans floretes; vol. 1, 2nd prologue).

The author of the collection of fables known by the name of *Isopet I-Avionnet* declares:

> Me voil traveillier et pener
> D'un petit jardin ahener
> Ou chascuns porra, si me samble,
> Cuillir et fruit et fleur ensamble. (ll. 7–10)

(I want to labor hard and endeavor to work a little garden where all will be able, it seems to me, to pick fruit and flower together.)

The flower represents the esthetic pleasure, the fruit is the moral profit, and he continues the metaphor by asking God for his dew "that will, by its grace, make the garden flower and bear fruit" (qui le jardinet, par sa grace,/Flourir et fructifier face).

The titles of numerous works are explicit as to the richness of this figurative field. Gardens and orchards designate collections, or *summae*, in a wide variety of domains: theological, as is *Le Jardin des Nobles* by Pierre des Gros (1464), or lyrical, as are *Le Jardin de Plaisance et fleur de rhétorique* published in 1501 by Antoine Vérard and the *Verger d'Honneur* by André de La Vigne.

Finally, the floral metaphor serves to reveal modes of composition. Jacques de Bugnin, in his *Congé pris du siècle seculier* (1480) assembles sayings "without putting them in piles like sheaves" (sans les mectre par monseaulx comme gerbes), he says, but groups them together "by couplets like special flowers" (par deux vers comme fleurs speciales).

Another metaphor that is frequently used compares the author to a demiurge. The central comparison is no longer with Nature, as in the preceding field, but directly with God, often represented as an architect, as is the God with a compass in a thirteenth-century *Bible moralisée* (Codex Vindobonensis 2554, fol. 1) preserved in the Austrian National Library in Vienna.[1] The metaphor emphasizes the composition of the works, their organization.

The Latin poetic arts insist that, just as a blueprint is necessary for erecting a building, a plan is essential to building a work. French authors come back to this precept. The work must be *compassée*. He who does not know how he will finish, should not begin. In his *Voir-dit,* Guillaume de Machaut recalls the proverb: "For we say that those who can see the end of their work work wisely" (Car on dit que sagement oeuvre/Cilz qui voit la fin de son oeuvre; ll. 8323–8324).

Eustache Deschamps enumerates the tools necessary for building specialists of all kinds: "Metalworker, carpenter, mason, painter, worker, writer" (Fevre, charpentier et maçon, /Paintre, manouvrier, escripvain), and concludes, as the refrain of his ballade: "One cannot work well without a ruler" (On ne peut bien sanz regle ouvrer; ballade 1364, vol. 7). This observation applies simultaneously to the material level and the moral level. All of the terms that Eustache uses can, in fact, have a double

interpretation: square, line, form, plumb line and, of course, ruler, all contribute to "leading the mason's work straight [to its goal]" (mener droit
[le] maçonnaige).

The different sections of a building are compared to the different parts
of a text in the process of its elaboration. Hugh of Saint Victor does this,
in Latin, in his *Didascalicon*. The foundations of the edifice represent the
historical meaning; the walls, the allegorical meaning; the interior with
its colors and its decor, the tropological meaning; the roof, the anagogi-
cal or eschatological meaning. The traditional origin of the architectural
metaphor is biblical, with symbolic commentaries about the Temple of
Solomon or the Ark of the Covenant. The same comparison exists, transposed, in French. Michault Taillevent, in his *Edifice de l'Hôtel douloureux
d'amour* (The Painful Structure of the Hotel of Love), describes the house
that Love has assigned to him:

> Le fondement est de merancolie
> Et les murs sont faiz de desconfiture,
> Le mortier est d'amere confiture
> Et puis aprez, afin qu'en hault se dresse,
> Il y a mis pour la maison conclure
> Comble de dueil et de dure destresse
>
> (ed. R. Deschaux, pp. 266–267)

(The foundation is of melancholy and the walls are made of failure,
the mortar is of bitter jam, and then after that, so that it rises up high,
to finish the house, there is an attic of grief and harsh distress.)

In the last line, the play on the word *comble* (attic) joins the literal sense
with the figurative, referring both to the top of the building and the height
of the pain. Also in this semantic field, the titles of the works are telling.
The text describes or becomes a castle: *Château d'amour* (Castle of Love)
by Robert Grosseteste (circa 1215), *Chastel perilleux* (Perilous Castle) by
Frère Robert the Carthusian, at the end of the fourteenth century, *Chasteau de Labour* (Castle of Labor) by Pierre Gringore (1499), *Chasteau
d'Amours* by the same author (1500); a city: *Livre de la Cité des Dames*
(Book of the City of Ladies) by Christine de Pizan; a room (*salle*): such
is the title that Antoine de la Salle, playing with his own name, gives to
one of his collections; a temple: *Temple d'Honneur et de Vertu* (Temple

of Honor and Virtue) by Jean Froissart, *Temple de Bocace* (Temple of Boccaccio) by George Chastelain, *Temple d'Honneur* (Temple of Honor) by Jean Lemaire de Belges; or a house: *Maison de Conscience* (House of Conscience) by Jean Saulnier (after 1413). Architecture and allegorical imagination weave tight bonds, and we can follow the intertextual links that use this register. For example, Antitus, chaplain of the dukes of Burgundy and Savoy, wrote a *Portail du Temple de Bocace* (Portal of the Temple of Boccaccio), after Georges Chastellain's text.

Other metaphors that link artisan crafts to writing can be found. The writer calls himself a potter, a blacksmith, or a weaver, even a cook. The work of the writer that, in a nature metaphor, is called *enter* (to graft) may be expressed in culinary terms with the verbs *entrelarder* or *farcir* (to lard or to stuff). The desired goal in both cases is beauty and savor.

Finally, writing is seen as a type of navigation. The metaphor goes back to Antiquity and is very frequent in Latin literature of the Middle Ages, in particular in St. Jerome. Writing has a goal, and it must arrive safely: "May we be able to drop anchor at a safe port" (Qu'a dreit port puisse ancre geter), Benoît de Sainte-Maure exclaims in the middle of his *Roman de Troie* (l. 14950). This formula is found throughout the Middle Ages and becomes a conclusory turn of phrase. The image is reinforced by the word *rimer*, which has a double meaning in Old French: to rhyme and to row. Gerbert de Montreuil plays with this in the conclusion of his *Roman de la Violette*:

Gyrbers de Mosteruel define
De la Vïolete son conte,
N'en velt plus faire lonc aconte,
Tant a rimé k'il est a rive.   (ll. 6634–6637)

(Gerbert de Montreuil [here] concludes his tale of the Violet and no longer wishes to tell more. He has rhymed/rowed so much that he has arrived at the shore.)

The images and the forms are linked. The medieval reverie about the word *rime* proves it.

CHAPTER SEVEN

Modes of Composition

Numeral Patterns

Rhetoric gives only very general indications as to the composition of a work. Numeral patterns were therefore a powerful resource in the Middle Ages. Behind this pattern can be found references to cosmology, to the Bible, and to folklore. The underlying principle, in fact, is the certitude that the world is well ordered. The author seeks to reproduce this same perfection. A composition of this type has a double value: a structural value and a symbolic value according to the number retained.

Subtle studies have been conducted to analyze, according to this principle, the structure of the first hagiographic legends. Eleonor Webster Bulatkin has asserted that the *Vie de saint Alexis* is organized around the number five and its powers, and can be interpreted with the help of this number's symbolism. Cesare Segre has analyzed the *Chanson de sainte Foy* (Song of Saint Fides) and shown that it is composed of five periods of eleven stanzas. The numeral organization stands out in Dante's *Divine Comedy* where the three times thirty-three songs, plus one, in *Inferno*, that serve as a prologue, tell of the unity in the trinity.

Esthetically speaking, a few figures or numbers are especially significant. Round numbers are among these. *La Somme le roi* (The Book of Vices and Virtues) [by Frère Laurent d'Orléans, confessor to King Philippe le Hardi (1270–1285)] affirms this of the number 100:

> The number 100 is the most perfect, for it represents a round figure that is the most beautiful and most perfect among the others; for, just as in the round figure the end returns to its beginning and resembles in this way a crown, the number 100 joins the end to the beginning for 10 times 10 equals 100, which signifies the crown that crowns the Wise Virgins.

(Li nombres de .C. est li plus parfez, quar il represante une figure reonde qui est la plus bele et la plus parfaite entre les autres; quar, auxi come en la reonde figure la fin retorne a son comancement et fet auxi comme une corone, auxi li nombre de .C. joint la fin au comancement, quar .X. foiz .X. sont .C., qui senefie la corone qui les sages virges coronne.)

The number fifty functions in the same way. The numbers "one hundred" and "fifty" supply a "natural" ending for poems built in stanzas. *Les Vers de la mort* (Verses on Death) by Hélinand de Froidmont contains fifty stanzas. When lyrical poetry of fixed forms was transformed into stories in the fourteenth century, there began the emergence of collections of one hundred ballades: *Cent Ballades* and *Cent Ballades d'Amant et de Dame* by Christine de Pizan, *Cent Ballades* by Jean Le Seneschal and his friends, *Cinkante Balades* (Fifty Ballades) by John Gower.

This numeral organization also applies to the narrative genre: Boccaccio's *Decameron*, the *Cent Nouvelles Nouvelles*. And to didactic texts as well, like the *Epistre Othea* by Christine de Pizan, known also as *Cent Histoires de Troie* (One Hundred Stories of Troy).

The case of Martial d'Auvergne's fifty-one *Arrêts d'amour* (Love Judgments) is significant. Why fifty-one and not fifty? It seems that the supplementary unit, the fifty-first judgment, underlines the cyclic form of the work, its infinite movement that only an arbitrary decision can stop. In this case, the author uses not the round number, but a device that combines the tiredness of the presiding judge, "Who was weary and could go on no longer" (Qui estoit las et n'en povoit plus), the weak voice of the clerk who continues to pronounce the judgments that the author cannot hear and therefore record and, finally, his own tiredness: "And then my quill was very weary, which is why I couldn't understand a thing" (Et puis ma plume estoit fort lasse,/Par quoy n'eusse sceu rien comprendre).

Other numbers and figures play on symbolic values. The number three is characteristic of the outlines of tales and is found in texts such as *Le Dit des trois morts et des trois vifs* (The Tale of the Three Dead Men and the Three Live Ones), or with a comic effect founded on the use of repetition in the fabliaux. *Les Trois Dames qui troverent l'anel* (The Three Ladies Who Found the Ring), *Les Trois Bossus ménestrels* (The Three

Hunchbacked Minstrels), on the theme of the recalcitrant dead man, or *Constant du Hamel*, all work according to this principle.

The omnipresence of the number five is very instructive as this number combines religious motivations. There is the example of David's five stones in the Old Testament. In the New Testament there are Christ's five wounds and the five people at the foot of the cross. The number five has an arithmological value in that it is a combination of an even and an odd number: two, which is the number of woman and is imperfect because it can be divided, and three, the number of man, which refers back to the unity, to perfection. Finally, it has an anthropological value: the five senses of man, the five fingers on a hand.

The pattern of the five senses in the organization of medieval stories and texts is important. First of all, it can serve as a global model of organization. This is the case, for example, of Jean Baudouin's moral and historical compilation *L'Instruction de la vie mortelle* (The Instruction on Mortal Life), a text from the beginning of the fifteenth century. This 47,000-line work is divided into five parts referring back to the five senses. Other texts that are much shorter, such as *La Doctrine et Loz pour Madame Aliénor* (also known as The Five Senses), by Olivier de la Marche, use this model. More often, it is sections of works that are organized in reference to the senses. The didactic and moral teaching in the Reclus de Molliens' *Miserere* uses this five-part model across some forty stanzas. Similarly, a part of the confession in Pierre de Hauteville's *Confession et Testament de l'amant trespassé de deuil* uses this format. The principle is identical in the *Testament Pathelin*.

Finally, love's journey can be built according to a progression from one sense to another. These are the degrees of love, hierarchical, directed, that lead from love born of sight to the *fait* (act), the sexual act that corresponds to the sense of touch. This is the formula found in the lyrical poetry of the troubadours and in the *Romance of the Rose* as well. We get a glimpse of the link between this pattern and the organization of textual spaces according to a metaphorical coloring that can be variable, the pilgrimage, for example, or the hunt.

The process of composition by numbers leads to an enumerative construction that is the basis for many medieval texts and, in particular, short texts: *Dit des Neuf Preux* (Poem of the Nine Gallant Men), *Dit des Douze mois de l'année* (Poem of the Twelve Months of the Year), *Quinze*

Signes du jugement dernier (Fifteen Signs of the Last Judgment), *XV Joyes de Nostre Dame* (Fifteen Joys of Our Lady), *Quinze Joies de mariage* (Fifteen Joys of Marriage). A predilection for lists is one of the esthetic tendencies of medieval writing.

The Genealogical Principle

The number is a principle of discontinuous series; genealogy, however, functions in stories following the trend of chronology. This is found first of all in romance. Some texts, indeed, are constructed in a bipartite manner as in the history of a father followed by that of the son. This is the case of Chrétien de Troyes' *Cligès,* which covers two generations; that of the father, Alexander, son of the emperor of Constantinople, at King Arthur's court, and that of his son Cligès. It traverses two worlds: England and the East.

This formula appears often. Jean Renart, for example, builds his romance of the *Escoufle* on this model. He recounts the life of Richard de Montivilliers in Normandy, then the life of Richard's son, Guillaume, raised at the court of the emperor of Rome. In Robert de Blois' short story *Floris et Lyriope,* three generations are played out: Narcissus (the duke of Thebes), his daughter Lyriope, who falls in love with Floris, and their son, also named Narcissus, whose story is that of Ovid's Narcissus in the *Metamorphoses.*

Chronology and genealogy also serve to beget texts, to graft them onto model texts. These principles work like a motor of invention, in the *chanson de geste* as in the romance. Taking the story of a hero, Guillaume of the *Chanson de Guillaume,* for example, other stories are spun off about his adult years: *Couronnement de Louis, Charroi de Nîmes, Prise d'Orange, Aliscans*; and then the stories of his childhood are added: *Enfances Guillaume*; and of his old age: *Moniage Guillaume* (he becomes a monk), in a way that recreates the story of a life from youth to old age. Not only the life of the hero can be played out, but also that of his lineage. Every epic or romance hero gives birth, then, to the story of his father, of his grandfather, of his ancestor, according to the formula "the sons have begotten the fathers": Garin de Monglane, in the case of Guillaume, and Florimont, Alexander the Great's great-grandfather, in Aimon de Varenne's eponymous romance. The sons give us the stories of the fathers.

The Arthurian romance *Guiron le Courtois* brings to life the generation before that of the principal knights of the Round Table: Meliaduc, father of Tristan; Lac, father of Erec; Pellinor, father of Perceval; and, of course, Uther Pendragon, father of Arthur. And from the fathers, we gain entry into the stories of the sons. After having followed the different adventures of Gawain, we can become attached to those of his son, Gingalain, in *Le Bel Inconnu* (The Fair Unknown). The romance of *Ysaÿe le Triste* from the fourteenth century imagines a son of Tristan and Yseut, born of adultery: Ysaÿe. It tells the story of Ysaÿe and his son, Marc. Onomastically, from King Marc, Yseut's husband, to her grandson Marc, the circle is completed by paths where, in the line of descent, bastardy and legitimacy overlap.

Tales can give preference to horizontal expansion over vertical proliferation and can privilege, not the fathers or the sons, but collateral relatives. This phenomenon is observed in the epic genre, for example, with Vivien, Guillaume d'Orange's nephew and hero of the *Chevalerie Vivien* and of the *Enfances Vivien*; or in the *Roman de Renart*, where Primaut, Ysengrin's brother, reenacts the theft of the herrings. It is a human genealogy, but it pertains to a very specific object: the Grail. *Le Roman de l'estoire dou Graal* (*Merlin and the Grail: Joseph of Arimathea, Merlin, Perceval*), a short cycle supposedly by Robert de Boron, recounts the Grail's transfer from the East to the West. This is the aim of all of the prose cycles that bring together the story of the relic and the future of the descendants of Joseph of Arimathea, including the *Lancelot-Grail* and even the *Prose Tristan*. In fact, Tristan's ancestor, Apollo, is presented as the great-nephew of Joseph of Arimathea.

Finally, tales can multiply through crossbreeding; of lineages and of subject matters. Auberon, in *Huon de Bordeaux*, is the son of Julius Caesar and Morgan le Fay, sister of King Arthur. This melds together Arthurian and classical subject matter, and even hagiography, since St. George is Auberon's twin brother. Galien, in *Galien le Restoré*, is the son of Olivier and Jacqueline (daughter of the emperor Hugon of Constantinople). Eastern and Western worlds join together in this work, in which the *Chanson de Roland* and the *Pèlerinage de Charlemagne* intersect. Lastly, *Perceforêt* unites the adventures of Alexander and the quest for the Grail. Renewal takes the form of concretion, a synthesis of immense materials, a totalizing desire to embrace the entire universe.

Continuations

Due to a chance of history or a deliberate will to incompletion, many texts are presented as interrupted, awaiting a continuation or an ending. This is the case of the *Knight of the Cart*. Chrétien entrusts its ending, the part that follows Lancelot's imprisonment in the Tower by Meleagant, to Godefroy de Lagny, who comments in his intervention: "He did it with the approval of Chrétien" (ç'a il fet par le boen gré/Crestïen; ll. 7106–7107). Gautier de Belleperche, who began his *Roman de Judas Macchabé* at an advanced age, is interrupted some 23,000 lines before Judas's end. The poem is finished by Piéros du Riés who tells of Judas's death. The incompletion of the *Story of the Grail* by Chrétien de Troyes leads to a whole series of continuations in verse: the anonymous first continuation, or *Continuation-Gauvain*; Wauchier de Denain's second, or *Perceval Continuation*; Manessier's third; and Gerbert de Montreuil's fourth. Such is the call of the mystery, the desire to see the sword from the Grail procession mended, to fill in the *creveüre*, the cracks both in the object and in the text. Jean de Meun assumes the role of continuer, forty years later, of the *Romance of the Rose* by Guillaume de Lorris, who was taken by death: "for where Guillaume stops, Jean will continue it, after his death" (car quant Guillaumes cessera,/Jehans le continuera,/enprés sa mort; ll. 10557–10559). Guillaume de Lorris had carried the love quest to the fourth degree, the kiss, that is, taste, according to the regimen of the senses; Jean de Meun, at the end of an inspired philosophical amplification, gets him to the fifth degree, the *fait* (act), touch: "Thus I had the scarlet rose. Then it was day and I woke up" (Ainsint oi la rose vermeille./Atant fu jorz, et je m'esveille; ll. 21749–21750).

In Old French this exhausting of a subject in the desire to bring it to an end, to *finish* it off, is called *parfaire* (to perfect). Godefroy de Lagny uses this term in naming his geste: "The clerk Godefroi de Leigni has perfected the *Charrette*" (Godefroiz de Leigni, li clers,/A parfinee la charrete; ll. 7102–7103).

The texts that appear in connection with the *Voeux du Paon* (Vows of the Peacock) show the various possibilities for pursuing a matter. To begin with, the first text, *Les Voeux du Paon* by Jacques de Longuyon, is grafted onto a subject matter, that of Alexander. Jacques' text remains open-ended because one of the vows (*voeux*) that a young lady made has not been accomplished by the end of the work. Edeas had, indeed, sworn to restore in gold the animal upon which the vows were pronounced during the banquet. Jean le Court dit Brisebare thus takes up the story explicitly at this point. Speaking of his predecessor, he writes: "And he who put it in verse, this was no feat, forgot this restoration, but I have very seriously grafted it on after the death of Clarvus of the country of the Amazons" (Et cils qui le rima, ce ne fu pas esplois,/Oublia cel restor, mais je l'ai sans gabois/Enté aprés la mort Clarvus le Mazonois; ll. 66–68). From the point of view of poetic practice the two important terms are *oublia* (forgot) and *enté* (grafted). The continuation fills in a gap with a graft. The *Restor du Paon*, as the work is named, is both a recreation, through the art of goldsmithing, of the dead peacock, and the creation of a text by this name. The third author, finally, Jean de le Mote, undertakes to perfect (*parfaire*) the work of his predecessors from a formal point of view. Jacques de Longuyon commenced the *Voeux du Paon*, creating the beginning, Jean le Court completed the middle part (*le moilon*), and Jean de le Mote will fashion the best extremity, "le meilleur coron" (ll. 14–15).

As for the theme, his predecessors having used marriage and death in their sections, he turns to the notion of vengeance: he will tell of the vengeance of King Clarvus's death. The idea of vengeance is, in fact, a principle of continuation that adds the dimension of causality to that of chronological succession. Many medieval texts include the word "vengeance" in their titles, and this in all types of subject matter: the subject of Alexander in the *Vengement Alexandre* by Gui de Cambrai and the *Venjance Alixandre* by Jean le Névelon; religious subject matter in the *Vengement Nostre Seigneur*, in reference to the *Passions*; Arthurian subject matter in the *Vengeance Raguidel*; and epic subject matter in the *Vengeance Fromondin* in the *Geste des Lorrains*.

To continue, to fill in a gap, to saturate the tale, and, in order to do this, to write a new *branch* of it, is the model of composition chosen by the various authors of *Renart*. The second among them, in order to be able to take over, accuses his predecessor, Pierre de Saint-Cloud, of having left out "the best of his matter" (le mieux de sa matière), "For he forgot the process and the judgment that were rendered as to the enormous fornication of Renart" (Car il entroblïa le plet/Et le jugement qui fu fet/ . . . /De la grant fornicacïon/Que Renart fist), he tells us. Motivating an entire literature is the notion that writing in branches indicates tastes and success.

CHAPTER EIGHT

Models of Writing

S OME LARGE FIELDS OF KNOWLEDGE serve to define didactic, satiric, or parodic texts. This type of writing generally combines a vocabulary that is supplied by the chosen intellectual model, and a formal mold.

The Grammatical Model: Donats and Doctrinals

Ernst Robert Curtius discussed the use of grammatical metaphors since the end of Antiquity, and Paul Lehmann's *Parodie im Mittelalter* (Parody in the Middle Ages) offers examples of these scholarly pleasantries in Latin. They are also to be found in medieval French literature, and are not limited there to the clerical domain. Charles of Orleans addressed a mischievous rondeau to his secretary Estienne le Goût, built around this metaphor: "Master Etienne le Goût, nominative, newly on the optative mode wanted to be copulative. But his genitive case failed him" (Maistre Estienne le Gout, nominatif,/Nouvellement par maniere optative/Si a voulu faire copulative;/Mais failli a en son cas genitif; rondeau 83). The secretary responded to him in the same register. The phenomenon can be observed on a large scale as well.

The term "donat" signifies grammatical compendiums inspired by the tradition of the *Ars minor* of the Latin grammarian Aelius Donatus (second half of the fourth century CE). These compendiums, in the true sense, are numerous. Modeled on Uc Faidit's *Donatz Proensals*, which proposes an overview of metrics and a grammar of the langue d'oc, treatises were written that preserved the form of the grammatical textbook but transposed the subject matter into different fields. Among these, we may note Jean Gerson's *Donat de dévotion*, or *Donatus spiritualis*, evidently translated and printed by Colard Mansion after 1479, and the *Donet baillié au roy Loÿs Douzieme* by Jean Molinet, which is also to be found under the title *Donnet baillé au feu roy Charles huytiesme de ce nom*.

A similar transposition is seen with Alexandre de Villedieu's *Doctrinale*, a grammar textbook that was popular in the schools of the Middle Ages, of which there are more than four hundred extant manuscript copies.

In 1466, Pierre Michault, aware that Alain de Lille is playing with grammatical vocabulary in his *De planctu Naturae* (The Complaint of Nature)—he cites it under the title *Des plaintes de Nature* (Complaints of Nature)—produced a *Doctrinal du temps present* (Doctrinal of the Present Day) entirely founded on a parodic confusion of grammar and vice. Accompanied by Virtue, the narrator visits a school of Vices, whose general rector is Fausseté (Falseness). Twelve masters teach there. *Vantance* (Boasting), for example, explains the cases of declension: the nominative, his own name; the genitive, that of his ancestors, those who have engendered him. *Concupiscence* exposes the genres, *Hic*, *Hec*, *Hoc*, masculine, feminine, neutral. *Corruption* leads the chapter on short and long vowels.

But many texts that are called *Doctrinal* in the Middle Ages do not play with grammatical vocabulary but simply dispense a teaching, a doctrine. This is so for the *Doctrinal des Princesses et nobles dames, faict et deduict en XXIII rondeaulx* (Doctrine for Princesses and Noble Ladies, Written and Deduced in XXIII Rondeaux) by Jean Marot, and for very many short texts from the end of the fifteenth and the sixteenth centuries, addressing the different states, for example: *Doctrinal des filles à marier* (Doctrine for Girls to Be Married) and *Doctrinal des bons serviteurs* (Doctrine for Good Servants).

Some treatises can simultaneously function as such on a matter that they discuss in a literal sense and apply metaphorically to another domain. This happens in the *Leys d'Amors* at the beginning of the fourteenth century. In the prose version in five books—the first redaction—we find grammar, poetics, parts of discourse, rhetoric, and rhymes. However, through this rich homologous reflection on harmony, the eight parts of discourse are compared with the different social categories. In discussing the verb, it asserts, "the verb, in the manner of an emperor or a great king, wants to govern and does not want to be governed" (le verbs a maniera d'emperador o de gran rey, vol regir e no vol esser regitz). Any treatise, however technical, leads to a vision of the society and of the world.

The Religious Model

Religion provided efficient formats or molds, in the shape of its universally familiar manuals and breviaries, into which other subject matter could be poured, whether parodic or not. At the end of the thirteenth century, for example, the jurist Maître Ermengaud de Béziers compiled a vast *Breviari d'Amour* (Breviary of Love) based on a representation of the tree of love and of its ramifications, a painting that appears at the beginning of the manuscripts. His plan allows him to go from the love of God (a section in which he comments, for example, on the Credo) to the love of a man and a woman, the last part, in which he abundantly quotes the poetry of the troubadours. In this way, his book becomes a sort of museum of past lyrical poetry.

In the fifteenth century, Alain Chartier composed a *Breviaire des nobles* (Breviary of Noblemen), consisting of thirteen ballades and concluding with a rondeau. The first ballade, placed in the mouth of *Noblesse* (Nobility), affirms the title of breviary in its refrain that enjoins the reader: "May he say his daily prayers in this breviary" (Ses heures die en cestui breviaire). The twelve other ballades recall the virtues that must characterize the estate of *Noblesse* and the duties of the nobles, of *Foy* (Faith) and *Sobriété* (Temperance). Continuing the metaphor a few years later, Michault Taillevent pursues the teaching intended for nobles in his *Psautier des villains* (Psalter of Peasants): "Of the nobles I have seen the breviary that Master Alain made formerly, in his time" (Des nobles j'ay veü le brevïaire: Que fist jadis en son temps maistre Allains). His teaching is identical: one is only "villain" (peasant) in heart. The structure is similar: a ballade by the *acteur*, the author, the master of the game, introduces twelve ballades placed in the mouth of virtues, from *Gentillesse* (Honor) to *Bonne Renommée* (Good Renown).

On the model of the Gospels, which were not translated into French until the thirteenth century, such as, for example, *Les Evangiles des Domées* (The Sunday Gospels), the Middle Ages produced a certain number of satirical texts entitled *Evangiles,* among them an *Evangile aux femmes* (Gospel for Women), known in several versions, from the end of the thirteenth century, and *Evangiles des quenouilles* (Gospels of the Distaffs) from the end of the fifteenth century. In these titles, the parodic intention is obvious. There is a sort of oxymoron: a woman's word can only be the opposite of the gospel truth! The *Evangiles des quenouilles* opens with an insistence on a parallel with the Christian Gospels. The text even justifies, in a comical way, the number of women who are going to speak: six, compared to the four Evangelists, by using a misogynistic proportion that pretends to be serious: "And for that which, in all testimony of truth, it is suitable to have three women for two men" (Et pour ce que en tout tesmoingnage de verité, il convient trois femmes pour deux hommes . . .). This travestied arithmetic participates in the parody. All of the prayers are represented by parodic versions, in particular, the Our Father: *Patrenostre d'Amours* (Our Father of Love), *patrenostre à l'userier* (Our Father of the Usurer), *patrenostre du vin* (Our Father of Wine), but also the Joys of the Virgin echoed by the satiric text of the *Quinze joies de mariage* (Fifteen Joys of Marriage). The *Sermons joyeux* (Joyful Sermons), dramatic texts for a single voice, from the fifteenth and sixteenth centuries, playfully reproduce the structure of a sermon by transferring it from the wording of the theme to the development. The domains that can be put on the same level as religion are those that matter in the profane world: love, woman, money, wine.

Finally, texts copy practices such as the confession: John Gower's *Confessio Amantis* (Lover's Confession) in the fourteenth century, Pierre de Hauteville's *Confession et Testament de l'amant trespassé de deuil* (Confession and Testament of the Lover Who Died of Grief), and the fifteenth-century *Confession de la belle fille* (Confession of the Beautiful Girl).

The Juridical Model

All institutions that possess their own language, or code, supply models to literary writing. This is so for law, which offers vocabulary and modes of reasoning. Different formulae come out of it: debates, judgments, pleadings, trials.

Judgments appear in Andreas Capellanus's *The Art of Courtly Love* (between 1180 and 1186), in which they are attributed to noble ladies, such as Marie of Champagne, Eleanor of Aquitaine, and her mother, Ermengarde of Narbonne, among others.

The essential questions that are debated have to do with love. They could take on the sociological form of a debate between a cleric and a knight on the theme: "Who loves better, the cleric or the knight?" or discuss points of casuistry of love in a dialogue within a lyrical framework, which is what the *jeux partis* do. A context, a story, and even a dramatization can also be invented to present these questions.

The judgment of Paris served as an underlying model, and at times authors brought it up to date. Guillaume de Machaut wrote two judgments that answer each other on the theme: "Who is the most unhappy in love, the lover betrayed by his lady or the lady whose lover has died?" John I, count of Luxemburg and king of Bohemia [1296–1346], whose secretary was Guillaume de Machaut, decided in favor of the lover. The debate was then rejudged by the king of Navarre who condemned the poet to pay a poetic fine: to compose a lai, a virelai, and a ballade. In the *Confession de la belle fille*, the penitence imposed by the priest is also a poetic fine: not to compose but to recite four simple songs.

Though, at the beginning, the questions disputed in this type of text are essentially about love, they sometimes become political toward the end of the Middle Ages. The *Songe du Vergier* (Dream of the Orchard), offered to Charles V in Latin in 1376, and in French in 1378, creates a dialogue between a cleric and a knight about the respective powers of the pope and the king of France. Christine de Pizan's *Livre du Chemin de Longue Etude* (The Long Road of Learning) contains a political debate, before Reason, between four powers: *Noblesse* (nobility), *Chevalerie* (chivalry), *Richesse* (wealth) and *Sagesse* (wisdom). They debate the question of who should be entrusted with the governing of the world. The same goes for Alain Chartier's *Quadrilogue invectif* (1422). The three estates: the people, the knight, and the clergy, complain before a France in mourning, who complains as well.

The tone can also be lighter and the subjects can come under diverse topics of interest, such as the hunt, which also nevertheless touches on the question of nobility and love. In his prose treatise *Les Livres du Roy Modus et de la royne Ratio* (The Books of King Modus and Queen Ratio), written between 1354 and 1376, Henri de Ferrières inserts a poem of one thousand lines, a debate between two chatelaines about the question of which type of hunt is the most noble, with hounds or with hawks.

A few years later, Gace de la Buigne, chaplain of Jean le Bon, took up the question again in his *Romans des deduis* (Book of Pastimes) and staged a debate between *Amour des chiens* (Love of dogs) and *Amours d'oiseaux* (Love of Birds).

More and more professionals of justice turned to literary writing. Jean Le Fèvre's *Respit de la mort* (Respite from Death) and Martial d'Auvergne's *Arrêts d'Amour* (Rulings on Love) find their framework in juridical fictions. Though separated by almost one hundred years, both authors were prosecutors at the parlement of Paris. It is still in the juridical framework that the judgments brought about by the quarrel in Alain Chartier's *Belle Dame sans merci* (Beautiful Lady Without Pity) are situated.

The Testamentary Model

From the end of the thirteenth century to the middle of the sixteenth, the testament that combines the religious model and the juridical model made its way into everything: narrations, lyrical poetry, theater. It is even to be found autonomously in works that, from Eustache Deschamps to François Villon and to the dramatic parodies of the beginning of the sixteenth century, are called "testament."

The writing of the literary testament has two sides: a serious, even solemn one that links a code, the law, to a theme, death; and a comical side with a satirical aim that parodies the code and makes the theme laughable. The result is a tension between satire and lyricism, an expression of the *rire en pleurs* (laughing in tears) that is so characteristic of the time.

The testament implies a subject that gathers itself in the very act of bequeathing and then dissolves itself in death, striking a pose: sickness or old age. In doing so, the *testament* can appear as the emblem of a global esthetic for the literature of the last two centuries of the Middle Ages. It creates a *mise en abyme* of its own style of writing: writing in the first person founded on the absence of continuity, using formulae such as "I give" and *item,* it echoes the tensions that run through it; it tells its relationship to memory in this passionate desire to leave a mark.

PART THREE

Building the Sense

CHAPTER NINE

The Question of Literary Heritage

W**HAT ARE THE STAKES** in medieval literature from the point of view of meaning? How should their evolution be perceived? The binary characteristic of early medieval thought is striking, and one of the principal evolutions, within literature, is the complexification of this model. The binarism, first of all, is that of values that are put forth by the first *chansons de geste*. It can be summarized in these lines from the *Song of Roland*: "Pagans are wrong and Christians are right" (Paien unt tort e chrestïens unt dreit; l. 1015) or again "For we are right, but these gluttons are wrong" (Nos avum dreit, mais cist gluton unt tort; l. 1212).

This black-and-white perspective both typifies the ideology and affects the characters. Good guys against bad guys, loyal subjects against traitors, heaven opposed to hell.

Within groups, values are also split into pairs of opposition: "Roland is valiant and Olivier is wise" (Rollant est proz e Oliver est sage; l. 1093).

This way of thinking is not limited to one genre; it corresponds rather to a mentality, the feudal mentality. In the *Jeu d'Adam*, composed between 1146 and 1174, Adam, who has bitten into an apple, conscious of his sin towards his lord, God, cries out: "I cannot enter into argument with him, for I am wrong and he is right" (N'en puis contre lui entrer en plait,/Car jo ai tort, e il a droit; ll. 344–345).

In the *Testament*, Villon still attributes this type of thought to his mother, who sees paradise and hell painted in her church: "One scares me, the other brings me joy and happiness" (L'un me fait paour, l'autre joye et lïesse; l. 898), he has her say.

Binary thought goes hand in hand, for the well-read, with a taste for agonistic thought, encouraged by scholarly teaching and the academic exercise of *disputatio*. Texts entitled "battles" (*batailles*) or "tournaments" (*tournois*) proliferated, on the model of the psychomachy, or allegorical combat between virtues and vices, typified for medievals by Prudentius's

Psychomachia (fourth century CE). Examples include the *Bataille des sept Arts* (Battle of the Seven Arts); Henry d'Andeli's *Bataille des vins* (Battle of the Wines); and the *Bataille de Caresme et de Charnage* (Battle of Fasting and Carnival), which in a parody of the *chanson de geste* opposes Lenten fasting and its army of fish to the carnival's rich foods. We also have the *Bataille d'Enfer et de Paradis* (Battle of Hell and Heaven), where Paris and her allies, champions of heaven, confront Arras, upholder of hell, aided by Reims, Amiens, and Saint-Omer, in an allegorical battle.

On the model of the tournament, we find Huon de Méry's *Tournoiemenz Antecrit* (Tournament of the Antichrist), written between 1234 and 1240, and the *Tournoiement d'Enfer* (Tournament of Hell).

Texts whose titles advert to women's tournaments differ somewhat to the extent that they contain lyrical works: for example, Huon d'Oisy's *Le Tournoi des Dames* (c. 1180) and that of Richard de Semilli. The formula of the combat is pushed to the background to make room for an enumeration of ladies from a region or a city. This is the case of the *Tournoiement des dames de Paris* (The Tournament of the Ladies of Paris; c. 1270), a dit by Philippe le Bel's equerry Pierre Gencien, and of Jacques Bretel's *Tournoi de Chauvency*, an account of the celebrations held in Chauvency in 1285.

Warfare and love, an ancient binarism, define the romance of chivalry. One might hazard Jacques Roubaud's equation "*arma + amor* = Armor," arms plus love equal Brittany [l'Armorique].[1]

But if love pushes one to great feats in war, is this latter characteristic compatible with marriage? This is the debate that Chrétien de Troyes presents in *Erec et Enide* (c. 1170). Erec, accused of being "recréant d'armes," of neglecting warfare for the tranquility of a couple's love, must reaffirm his valiance through a series of trials. Beginning with the marriage of Erec and Enide, which appears at the end of a first section, whereas ordinarily marriage is—along with death—a conclusory formula for a tale, the work ends with the crowning of the two protagonists.

As with the battle scene, marriage is allegorized in the thirteenth century following the model of a greatly successful fifth-century text, Martianus Capella's *Marriage of Philology and Mercury*. Jean le Teinturier of Arras wrote a *Mariage of the Seven Arts* in which each discipline of the *trivium* and of the *quadrivium* marries a virtue or a theological practice.

Conversely, an anonymous author gives us a *Mariage des neuf filles du diable* (Marriage of the Devil's Nine Daughters). Here the offspring of the devil and *Mauvaistié* (Meanness) marry different social groups, which are therefore criticized. *Simonie* (Bribery) marries the prelates; *Hypocrisie* (Hypocrisy), the monks; *Rapine* (Thief), the knights; *Usure* (Usury), the bourgeois; *Tricherie* (Cheating), the merchants; *Sacrilège*, the laymen; *Faux-Service* (False-Service), the provosts and bailiffs; *Orgueil* (Pride), the ladies and maidens; and *Lècherie*, (debauchery) gives herself to all. This model is found in Latin as early as the beginning of the thirteenth century in texts by authors of sermons, such as Jacques de Vitry. Matheolus (Matthieu le Bigame), at the end of the thirteenth century, uses it in the second book of his *Lamentations*, which were translated by Jean Le Fèvre in the fourteenth century. Marriage brings together that which battle separates. But in both cases, it is a question of couples. The satirical discourse of the "*bestournement*," the overturned world, remains within this pattern: "Right has become wrong" (*Drois est devenu tors*), Eustache Deschamps deplores in the fourteenth century (ballade 803, 3:371).

From Symbol to Sign

And yet, as early as the end of the twelfth century, a more complex way of thinking, which blurs frontal oppositions to the benefit of a perspective on the paradoxical, progressively developed. People realized that "opposite things" (*contraires choses*), to use vocabulary from Jean de Meun's *Romance of the Rose*, are not simply in opposition with each other, but they interdefine each other as well: "Thus things go by contraries, one is the gloss of the other" (Ainsinc va des contreres choses,/Les unes sunt des autres gloses; ll. 21543–21544).

Drawing *distinctiones*—philosophical distinctions—led to an essential discovery, that of intermediary states. As Charles d'Orléans' formula from the fifteenth century says: "Neither good nor bad, but between the two" (Ne bien ne mal, mais entre deulx; rondeau 286, ed. J.-C. Mühlethaler). In the religious domain, it was the promotion of Purgatory according to the fruitful analyses by Jacques Le Goff. In the literary domain, pushed farther and farther, the exploration was that of the interspace between sleeping and waking, with the enhancement of states like the *dorveille* (a combination of *dormir*—to sleep—and *veiller*—to be awake); the space between joy and pain with the presence of melancholy; between movement and immobility in the reflection on nonchalance; the space between places: between the castle and the forest—a third place—the moor; the space between times and sexes: this is one of the questions asked by metamorphosis or, in a lighter tone, the disguising of a person of the opposite sex.

There is also the diffraction of the subject: laughter in tears. In painting, it is the invention of the chiaroscuro of which we find a magnificent representation in a miniature at the opening of the Vienna manuscript version of René of Anjou's *Livre du Coeur d'amour épris* (Book of the Love-Smitten Heart). The light comes from a candle hidden in the foreground under a stool. This type of lighting goes hand in hand with the state of *dorveille* in which the main character finds himself "half asleep in a daydream" (moicité dormant en resverie; l. 38), a state favorable to dreaming.

An essential repercussion of these interrogations concerns the question of truth. Is there an interspace between truth and lie? The question has troubled minds for a long time. Just think of the ambiguous oath taken by Béroul's Yseut: nobody has ever been between her thighs, other than her husband, King Marc, and the leper who has just carried her across the muddy ford (in fact, Tristan in disguise). Gottfried of Strasbourg was scandalized by this formal truth some fifty years later.

Such is the problem that fiction poses, "Neither completely a lie, nor completely the truth, nor entirely madness, nor entirely wisdom" (Ne tut mençunge, ne tut veir,/Tut folie ne tut savoir; ll. 9793–9794), according to Wace in the *Roman de Brut*. This becomes an essential preoccupation when ambiguity, with Charles V, who was known for drawing up ambiguous treaties, becomes a way of waging war. Expressions gain power, like the one used by Jean de Meun to qualify the stupefaction of Pygmalion before his statue that has come to life: "he doesn't know if it is a lie or the truth" (ne set se c'est mançonge ou voir; l. 21110). One may worry over or delight in seeing a conscious display of the desire to deceive, to "make black out of white," a formula that defines the art of Renart.

More and more often situations are exposed in which indecision is appropriate, where it is impossible to separate the true from the false. This is the process that Guillaume de Machaut emphasizes by means of dreams within the text of his *Voir-dit*. What do these dreams tell him? Is his lady deceiving him? The infinite *mise en abyme* prohibits any logical conclusion. The only course of action that remains for the lover is the bet. He must bet on faithfulness—it is the moral duty in a work that claims to be in praise of ladies—or behave as if he is betting on it.

We go from a world where, without hesitation, white is distinguished from black to a world where white and black are mixed into a color that is receiving more and more attention. In his fifteenth-century *Exposition des couleurs*, Jean Robertet makes the color gray speak:

> Je qui suis gris signiffie esperance,
> Coulleur moyenne de blanc et noir meslée;
> Et soye seulle ou à autre assemblée,
> Le moyen tiens en commune actrempence.

> (I who am gray signify hope, a middle color, mixed from white and black; and alone or united with another, I stand in the middle in a common moderation.)

The gray of hope becomes little by little the gray of sadness. When interpreting the term *moyen* [middle, average, mediocre], it is all a matter of point of view.

Chrétien de Troyes presents the strange head of the horse that Enide receives from Guivret as having a white cheek and a black cheek: "Between the two there was a line, greener than a vine leaf, that separated the black from the white" (Entre deux avoit une ligne/Plus vert que n'est fuelle de vigne,/Qui departoit le blanc dou noir; ll. 5319–5321).

As the centuries pass, the line that separates is replaced by a blending or an impossible demarcation. In the thirteenth century, terms that existed in medieval Latin but that are not found in twelfth-century French begin to appear. The use of these terms begins to develop especially in the fourteenth century. The word *ambiguïte* (ambiguity) appears as early as the thirteenth century, and *ambigu* (ambiguous) is found in Christine de Pizan. In Bersuire's work, from the early fourteenth century, we find *perpelexité* (perplexity) and *perplexe* (perplexed). The history of vocabulary testifies strongly to an evolution.

Disjunction and Non-Disjunction

The Middle Ages were characterized by a firm belief in the existence of well-defined social positions, in statuses intended by God. A person's nature must not be transgressed, his condition must not be exceeded. Clerics stood opposite knighthood, and each pole corresponded to clearly defined values. On the side of the knights, there are weapons, on the side of the clerics, scholarship, Latin, and knowledge. Yet, over the centuries, literature works toward uniting that which ideology separates, and this polarization, in its strict diametrical form, slowly dissolves.

In the Occitan romance *Flamenca*, Love encourages the hero to love by saying to him: "For you are a knight and a cleric" (Car tu es cavalliers e clercs; l. 1799). Back in the eleventh century, the *Vie de saint Alexis* introduced its Roman hero specifying that he had received an excellent education before going on to serve the emperor. From this indication, the author of *Tombel de Chartrose*, in the fourteenth century, who inserts in his collection a *Vie de saint Alexis*, makes an important addition, which he calls a "digression," to the effect that this usage is no longer in favor, that the princes and nobles of his time are more interested in having their children listen to "la gent Fauvel" (that is, deception) than to the clerics. He advocates the union of "knowledge with knighthood" (scïence o chevalerie; l. 164), knowledge that is not harmful to weapons. He alleges examples of great "educated" kings: Alexander, David, Caesar, and Charlemagne. Eustache Deschamps continues this teaching. "For knights are ashamed of being clerics" (Car chevaliers ont honte d'estre clers), that is, of being scholars, the refrain of one of his royal songs deplores (piece 401, 3:187). Arms and letters, "one and the other are good together" (l'un et l'autre est bon ensemble; l. 33), the epilogue to *Isopet I* affirms.

But in return, this non-disjunction of values blurs social distinctions. Arms and love no longer characterize solely the noble class. The proverb that Guillaume de Machaut recalls in the beginning of the *Fontaine amoureuse*: "A knight who is a coward and a cleric who wishes to be brave are not worth a handful of straw" (Chevalier acouardis/Et clers qui vuet estre hardis/Ne valent plein mon pong de paille; ll. 133–135) is demolished, to start with—at least in a dream—by the poet himself.

Miscastings appear. The abbot in the *Petit Jehan de Saintré* by Antoine de la Sale beats the knight in the domain of love (the lady of the

Belles Cousines accords her preference to him). At first, he is on top in an unchivalrous, barehanded fight. The abbot only loses when the battle is fought with noble weapons. In *Valentin et Orson*, a romance in prose from the end of the fifteenth century, two people—the archbishop who slandered the queen and the merchant who saved her—who by their function, according to ancient values should have no legitimate reason to fight, engage in a trial by combat, with God as judge, to decide the fate of the victim. Weapons are no longer the privilege of the knight, letters are no longer the privilege of the cleric. It is the dream of the philosopher-king that the author of the *Roman de Dolopathos* forcefully affirms.

Ambiguous Powers

The definition of love in the lyric, the romance, the arts of love, relies on a figure of style that speaks of the very nature, ambiguous as it is, of this power: the alliance of opposites, what rhetoric calls in Latin the *coincidentia oppositorum*. The definition is psychological and moral: love is cold and hot, joy and pain, good and bad. In the *Romance of the Rose*, Jean de Meun, who is following a passage from Alain de Lille's *De planctu Naturae*, gives this description to the lover: "Love, it is hateful peace, it is hate in love, it is disloyal loyalty and loyal disloyalty" (Amors, ce est pez haïneuse,/Amors, c'est haïne amoureuse;/c'est leautez la desleaus,/c'est la desleautez leaus; ll. 4263–4266). This delirium of ambiguity, which stretches over twenty lines, has all the more power in that it is placed in the mouth of Reason. At the beginning of the romance, in the part that is attributed to Guillaume de Lorris, the narrator meets the Love god. The god is presented with his two quivers made of opposite materials—wood that is knotty for the one, and a polished, decorated wood for the other—and two sets of five opposite arrows. This description allows an analysis of the feeling and the situations of love, in a tradition that goes back to Ovid's *Metamorphoses*. The elements are singled out. With Jean de Meun, and in spite of the fact that Reason has bragged to the lover of untying for him the knot of love (l. 4259), readers, like the lover, find themselves facing the intrication of feelings that are the very essence of love.

Another figure of power receives the same treatment: Fortune. In his *Remède de Fortune* (The Cure of Ill Fortune), Guillaume de Machaut borrows the stylistic process used by Jean de Meun when evoking Love: "Fortune is hateful love, unhappy happiness" (Fortune est amour haïneuse/Bonneürté maleüreuse; ll. 1129–1130). Everything in the face of Fortune tells of her contradictory duality: her two faces—one benevolent, the other hideous, one turned forward, the other backward—and of course her wheel, which tells of individual and historic destinies.

Certain authors succeed in translating formally, through the organization of their tales, this movement of the wheel of Fortune. Guillaume de Machaut achieves this in his *Voir-dit*. But he also doubles this structure with a dual evocation of Fortune and her wheel at the end of the work.

Other authors resort solely to the illustrated figure. Jacquemart Gielée concludes his *Renart le Nouvel*: "The figure is the end of our book" (Li figure est fins de no livre; l. 7749). The complexity of these powers is a result of the fact that they cross two models: binarism, a model of succession, white and then black; and simultaneity, white in black. The word *chantepleure* (singsob) expresses this double postulation, demonstrating the creative thought process behind language. It simultaneously designates an object of everyday life: a sort of faucet in a barrel (the term evokes the noise of the liquid that is running), a psychological state, and a type of moral text. Interpreted as a succession, it denounces the action of Fortune, who makes one who has just sung cry.

Rutebeuf focuses on its moral use. Fortune's victims may be dubbed Chantepleure: "In short, he had the name Chantepleure" (En cort term a non Chantepleure; *De Monseigneur Ancel de L'Isle*, l. 40), "And so they will have the name Chantepleure" (Lors auront il non Chantepleure; *Complainte de Constantinople*, l. 178). In the form of a proverb, sermons recall: "Mieux vaut pleure chante que chante pleure," it is better to cry first and to sing afterwards than the opposite. Nicole Bozon organizes several of his *Contes moralisés* around this model. This moral vision places heaven on the horizon of a successful life. This is the reason that Dante calls his work a comedy, a divine comedy. Begun in pain, in hell, it ends in the joy of heaven.

But the same is not true for the domain of human love. Again, a proverb says it for us: "Love begins in joy and ends in pain" (Amours commencent en joie/Et fenissent en dolour). This is the movement that is revitalized by Christine de Pizan's love poetry and a book like the *Cent Ballades d'Amant et de Dame* (One Hundred Ballades of Lover and Lady). In the space created by a term and by the order of its components—to sing, to cry—a duality of forces is expressed, for which other analyses, with the help of the same term, place the emphasis on the radical intrication of the elements. Guillaume de Machaut, in the *Dit du Lion*, affirms: "Just like the *chantepleure*, it makes one very often sing and cry" (Aussi com la chantepleure/Fait que moult souvent chante et pleure; ll. 663–664). In essence, he who is turned into a poet by love is in this situation. Renaut de Beaujeu says so within a romance of chivalry, *Le Bel Inconnu*, which claims to be a prayer to his lady: "Alas! for her I die and for her I sing" (Las! por li muir et por li cant; l. 1270). How can complexity be expressed in writing?

The Dream

Right from the start, dreams appear in medieval texts of all kinds. Structurally, dreams are of two types: dreams by characters incorporated into a tale, such as the five dreams of Charlemagne in the *Song of Roland*, and dreams that function as the external structure of the text. I am concerned here with the latter category.

The advantage of presenting a text as a dream lies in several categories. The dream places the narrator in a central position and, at the same time, transforms him into a chosen one, a visionary, an inspired person. But this place is also kept in the background: to see in a dream is a little like seeing in a mirror, it is to gain access to an indirect vision. The dream combines speech in the first person with humility. In doing this, it protects the speaker, who can say anything critical he wants, since the dream filters his words, raising the question of whether it should be accorded the value of truth, and regarded as being of a prophetic nature, or seen as merely a lie.

As the external structure of a text, the dream is closely linked to the allegory. It allows two different uses, which sometimes work together: a political, social, moral criticism, in one case: and in the other, an exploration of states that, insofar as they do not represent reality, can escape pure reason and maintain their strangeness. In the first case, there are texts that, although not limited to this aspect alone, illustrate it perfectly: the *Songe d'Enfer* by Raoul de Houdenc, the *Romance of the Rose*, the *Advision Cristine* by Christine de Pizan, the *Quadrilogue invectif* by Alain

Chartier. In the second case, the dream opens itself up to exploration of the relationship between writing and the subconscious. "I will make a poem about pure nothingness" (Farai un vers de dreyt nien) writes Guillaume IX, who goes on, "I have just composed it in my sleep, on a horse" (Qu'enans fo trobatz en durmen/Sobre chevau; piece 4, ed. A. Jeanroy), or "I will make a poem since I am asleep" (Farai un vers, pos i sonelh; piece 5). The endpoint of these reveries that are reflections on poetic writing is found in short nonsense poems called *fatrasies*. The fifty-fourth *Fatrasie d'Arras* proclaims: "I versify while sleeping" (Je versefie en dormant).

Metamorphosis

Another phenomenon resulting from a reflection on complexity and that is intriguing and worrisome is metamorphosis. Does the reflection on the *mutacion* allow one to conceive of change, and in particular the change of shape? An underlying interrogation runs through the tales confronted with this question: were we already, in a latent manner, that which we are to become? Is metamorphosis the sign of a radical ambiguity of beings and things?

Two types of stories supply matter for reflection. There are the marvelous stories of folkloric origin, on the one hand, creating double beings: stories of werewolves or of knight-birds, which we find, among other places, in Marie de France; stories around [the water sprite] Melusine that are developed in the fourteenth century with Jean d'Arras' prose *Roman de Mélusine* and the versified version by Coudrette. On the other hand, the mythological stories taken from Ovid's *Metamorphoses*—Narcissus transformed into a flower, Daphne into a laurel tree, Actaeon into a deer, Arethusa into a fountain—present transformations that are all the consequence of a refused or impossible love. A profound link ties the dream to the metamorphosis in the way in which both pull away from the constraint and allow escape from misfortune through illusion or transformation.

The mythological figure that brings about this junction is that of Morpheus, the son of the god of sleep, "Who in several forms renews himself" (Qui en pluseurs formes se renouvelle), as Christine de Pizan characterizes him in one of her *Cent Ballades* (piece 42, l. 7). Present in the writings of Guillaume de Machaut, Eustache Deschamps, Christine de Pizan, and Geoffrey Chaucer, Morpheus exemplifies the powers of truth and illusion in dreams and metamorphoses. As a messenger, he reveals to sleepers truths that the latter still ignore—the death of the loved one in the example of Ceyx and Alcyone developed by Guillaume de Machaut in the *Fontaine amoureuse*, also called *Livre de Morpheüs* (Book of Morpheus). But he consoles by means of illusion, taking the form of the deceased. The example ends with the transformation of the two lovers into kingfishers (*alcyons*); the original form, having been lost, continues to exist in the name of the beloved.

At the beginning of the fourteenth century, the *Ovide moralisé* subjects these stories of metamorphosis by Ovid to a radical metamorphosis. It *converts* them from pagan stories into illustrations of Christian doctrine by means of what in the Middle Ages was called a "moralization," that is, an allegorical reading on several levels, the ultimate meaning of which is eschatological. It is a paradoxical method, contradictory even with the notion of metamorphosis, since it assigns a meaning to something in movement, to a reflection on creation that conceives of itself in the very act of transformation.

This method of reading was also applied to other texts, notably, that major thirteenth-century French verse romance *Le Roman de la Rose* [by Guillaume de Lorris and Jean de Meun], which at the end of the fifteenth century was "reduced" to prose and moralized by Jean Molinet. At the end of the fourteenth century, different *Echecs d'amour* in verse appear, as does a moralization in prose by Evrart de Conty. The moralization becomes a technique of writing. The meaning is built in a variety of ways between limitation with devices, such as that of moralization, and plasticity in the manipulation of the changing form that the metamorphosis emblematizes. At work here is the power of illusion, one of the powers of literature.

Allegory and Visual Games

Allegory, another significant process, plays an important role in the construction of the meaning of texts. The allegory is supported at times by graphic or visual games. The image of the game of chess is a good example, but it is not the only one. Everything could be allegorized in the

Middle Ages: animals, plants, objects. The domains from which the allegorical supports are borrowed are very diverse: the military domain, the religious or para-religious domain, any domain that fell under that of an art or a technique. Armor serves in this way as a comparative for Guiot de Provins in his *Armure du chevalier* (Armor of the Knight), and the sword for Jacques de Baisieux in his *Dit de l'Epée* (Dit of the Sword). There are multiple variations, giving form to entire works or inserted like fragments of a greater whole. A passage on the armor of the pilgrim in the *Pèlerinage de Vie Humaine* (Pilgrimage of Human Life) by Guillaume de Digulleville may serve as an example of the latter. Raoul de Houdenc allegorizes wings in his *Roman des Eles* (Romance of the Wings) just as Alain de Lille had done earlier in his *De sex alis Cherubim* (On the Six Wings of the Cherubim). The two wings of *Prouesse* (Valor): *Largesse* (Generosity) and *Courtoisie* (Galantry), have seven feathers apiece, which Raoul lists, that correspond to the qualities relevant to the wings that carry them. Guillaume de Machaut uses the Harp to speak in praise of his lady in the *Dit de la Harpe*: "I can very well compare my lady to the harp and adorn her beautiful body with the twenty-five strings that the harp has" (Je puis trop bien ma dame comparer/A la harpë, et son gent corps parer/De .XXV. cordes que la harpe a; ll. 1–3). Jean Froissart uses the clock and its mechanisms to analyze the springs of psychological life in his *Orloge amoureus* (Clock in Love): "I can easily compare myself to the clock" (Je me puis bien comparer a l'orloge; l. 1).

The method is always the same: the division of the object into its parts and the attribution of each part's *senefiance* (meaning, significance), its corresponding component in the moral or psychological world. The process is effective, both mnemonically, through its recourse to the list and to the visualization of the elements, and demonstratively. It is similar to the techniques called *ars memoriae* that are so remarkably analyzed by Frances Yates in her book *The Art of Memory* [1966]. It comes under the conviction held in the Middle Ages of a homology of the different levels that make up the world, of its profound harmony.

Allegorical analysis can be supported with diagrams or figures. In Matfre Ermengaud's *Breviari d'amor* (Breviary of Love), for example, the text opens with, follows, and comments on figures of a tree. Another tree appears in Robert de l'Omme's *Miroir de Vie et de Mort* (Mirror of Life and Death), a text in which the author underlines the didactic role of the figurative representation. The narrator sees in a dream a tree on which Life is perched, and he notices its roots: the roots of vice. Upon awaking from the dream, he specifies: "I was very afraid and nevertheless I had the tree painted right away so as to not forget it" (Grant peur oi, et nonpourquant/L'arbre fis paindre maintenant,/Ke je nel mesisse en obli; ll. 647–649).

More than one author thinks of the figure and the letter together, particularly in certain types of texts about didactic nature: bestiaries, like Philippe de Thaon's, and pilgrimages. In his *Pèlerinage de Vie Humaine* (The Pilgrimage of Human Life), Guillaume de Digulleville comments on the word PAX by writing the three letters that make it up in the form of a drawing of a carpenter's square: "as you see the figure of it" (si comme ci est figuré; l. 2526), he says.

The question of interpretation, in every sense of the word, is essential. It is fundamental in the performance of the texts, the musical execution in the case of the song, or the reading out loud for an audience, until well into the fourteenth century. Guillaume de Digulleville's *Pèlerinage de Vie Humaine*, in its first redaction, is conceived in days that correspond to sessions of reading. The first book ends with the formula: "You will come back another time if you wish to hear more about it" (Une autre fois vous revenres,/Se plus ouir vous en voulez; ll. 5063–5064). The second ends with: "I will take a break here. Come back tomorrow, if you want, and you will hear the continuation" (Et ci ferai une pausee. Demain, se voules, revenez/Et puis le remenant orrez; ll. 9046–9048). And the third with: "Come back another day, for here I will take a break" (Revenez une autre journee/Quar ci ferai une pausee; ll. 11405–11406).

There is a physical interpretation of texts and an intellectual one. The Middle Ages were passionately interested in the hermeneutic process, reflecting on the notion of gloss, or explication, conscious of its benefits and its dangers. Text and gloss: the couple is commented on ad infinitum, giving rise to expressions such as "to know neither text nor gloss" (ne connaître ni texte ni glose), serving to condemn folly. Among the dangers is the risk that the gloss will stifle or even destroy the text. The practices of the schools of Orléans, famous for their commentaries on ancient authors, gave rise to the saying "we freely admit that the gloss of Orléans destroys the text here" (on dit voulentiers que la glose/D'Orleans si destruit le texte). In Clément Marot's works, in the *Epistre du Coq à l'Asne faict par*

Lyon Jamet en l'an 1541, we find this comment: "It is a too obvious abuse to put forth gloss without text, like monks taking a crap" (C'est ung abus trop manifeste/Que d'alleguer glose sans texte,/Comme font les moynes crottez; ll. 142–144).

But the gloss, in the eyes of medieval writers, allows for a density of the text, the "strong" text, the text with a double meaning, "with two faces," in the expression of the time. It legitimates its obscurity, its strangeness, yet it is this obscurity that creates the desire to read. The gloss is there to explain, to develop that which the text envelops, encloses. *Complicatio* and *explicatio*.

There is a second benefit: it signals a conversation between texts. In a way it marks the development of what we call "literature." *Renart le Contrefait*, in the fourteenth century, reads the *Roman de Renart* and interprets it: "for about Renart we can gloss, think, study, dream" (car sur Regnart poeult on gloser,/Penser, estudier, muser; ll. 105–106). Earlier authors are glossed and, at the end of the Middle Ages, authors come to gloss their own texts.

Works are built on the play between invention and commentary. This is how Jean Froissart builds his *Prison amoureuse* [c. 1372], deploying the text on two levels: story and poems, and a commentary on these. Georges Chastellain followed up his 1457 verse *Dit de Vérité* (Poem of Truth), criticizing the French, with a prose *Exposition sur Vérité mal prise* (Exposition on Truth Misunderstood) explaining his misunderstood intentions. At the end of his *Testament*, a casually amused François Villon authorizes his executor—and beyond that, undoubtedly, his readers—to "gloss" and "comment on" it: "To interpret and give meaning, to his pleasure, better or worse" (Interpréter et donner sens/A son plaisir, meilleur ou pire; ll. 1857–1858). It is all about constructing or deconstructing the meaning. Villon's *Testament* raises the question of literary heritage—the question of literature.

Conclusion
The Incubation Period

In his beautiful book *Bild und Kult (Likeness and Presence)*, Hans Belting speculates about writing a "history of the image before the era of art." In this book, I have found myself in a position that, without being identical, presents certain analogies: writing a history of literature before the age of literature. My approach has been to question texts on their practice, to gather all that could be found of an implicit theory, all that could be understood of the authors, of the audiences, and of their tastes.

Medieval literature presents itself as an enigma. This either triggers rejection or inspires fascination. It is enigmatic first of all for contingent reasons: the distance that separates us from the language of that time, the change of customs and of the intellectual universe. This type of obscurity arises, in fact, for the reader or the observer at every point in history.

For Clément Marot in the sixteenth century, François Villon's fifteenth-century language had already become difficult to understand, and Villon's allusions to facts of daily life, to current events, were no longer accessible. Moreover, in giving the title *Ballade en vieux langage français* (Ballade in the Old French Language) to the poem that follows the *Ballades des Dames et des Seigneurs du temps jadis* (Ballades of Ladies and Lords of Yesteryear) in his edition of Villon, Marot expresses the feeling that Villon was sensitive to these variations in the state of the language and of style, and to the nostalgic poetry that could come of this. The refrain of the *Ballade en vieux langage français* is "Gone with the wind" (Autant en emporte ly vens).

This is a condition that I would gladly call the syndrome of "the Song of the Good King Henry" that Alceste, in [Molière's] *The Misanthrope*, opposes to Oronte's sonnet: "The rhyme is not rich and its style is old"

(La rime n'est pas riche et le style en est vieux). It is certainly true that a part of the difficulty and of the pleasure of reading medieval texts arises from this.

Also as a result of contingency are another difficulty and another pleasure that find their source in the obscurities of an altered transmission: lost voices, gnawing rats, sleeping scribes. The pleasure is then that of the hunter who tracks the difficulty the way one tracks a hare. The [textual] crux and *locus desperatus* (hopelessly corrupt passage) anguish and excite the philologist. But "signs," "tracks," and "trail marks" are also a pleasure for any reader, the pleasure of the quest for meaning. In a way that is no longer contingent, but essential, medieval literature asks the question of clarity or of obscurity as an esthetic principle. For the troubadours, it is the debate between *trobar lei* (clear) and *trobar clus* (closed) that opposes Guiraut de Borneilh and Raimbaut d'Orange in a famous *tenson*. The question of intentional obscurity feeds the reflection on literature, from the prologue of Marie de France's lays to Boccaccio's reflections in his *Life of Dante* to Philippe de Mézières' or Evrart de Conty's remarks. Obscurity leads readers to deeper meaning and engraves texts in memory. The *trobar clus* of the poet brings about the reader's happiness in making the find.

The debate about love, love that, under different forms, is at the root of writing—from the love of the lady to the love of knowledge and to the love of God—marks this awareness of the literary act. The following question is posed: is it possible to sing without love and, if so, is it legitimate? Gilles de Vieux-Maisons in his piece *Chanter m'estuet, car pris m'en est corage* (I Must Sing for I Desire to Do So), risks the solution that is not retained by his colleagues, Gace Brulé and Conon de Béthune in particular: "and I will sing without love, out of habit" (Si chanterai sanz amors, par usage).

The question is, then, how to write when the lady does not respond to one's love, or, in an extreme case, when she is dead. The solution of the courtly poets up to and including Guillaume de Machaut is to resort to a virtue, an allegorical power: hope. The poet is not loved but hopes to be loved, and this hope allows him to write. Yet, he writes in a degraded form because it is no longer anything but formulae, "pure affectation" in the terms of Alceste. It is what Oronte's sonnet says: "Beautiful Philis, we despair, although we still hope" (Belle Philis, on désespère, / Alors qu'on espère toujours).

To salvage the possibility of writing, the poets who come after Guillaume de Machaut emphasize the role of memory. Jean Froissart thus turns to artifacts—a mirror in which is reflected the lady in the *Espinette amoureuse* and a portrait in the *Joli Buisson de Jonece*—that allow him by means of a dream to reanimate a buried love.

But the ultimate solution is to change the nature of love. This is the writing of the *Divine Comedy* for Dante after the death of Beatrice, it is the end of Jean Froissart's *Joli Buisson de Jonece* where love no longer addresses the lady but the Virgin. In light of such a principle of writing, an unprecedented case arises when the lady not only refuses to grant her love—that would be banal or predictable—but even so much as the hope of love. This is the—very noisy—scandal caused by Alain Chartier's *La Belle Dame sans mercy* (The Beautiful Lady Without Pity). The lady does not feel responsible for the love that she has inspired. Her formula "eyes are made for looking" (les yeux sont faits pour regarder) transforms the very source of the spark of love into a simple optical organ, signaling a rupture and triggering a quarrel. Who is right or wrong—the lover who is dying from this refusal or the lady who is insensitive, but free?

In an *Excusation envers les dames* (Apology to Ladies), Chartier shields himself behind his characters, crying out:

S'en doibt tout le monde amasser
Contre moy, a tort et en vain,
Pour le chetif livre casser
Dont je ne suis que l'escripvain?   (ll. 213–216)

(Must everybody unite against me, wrongly and without cause, to suppress the mediocre book of which I am merely the scribe?)

Baudet Herenc submits *Accusations contre la Belle Dame sans Mercy* (Charges Against *La Belle Dame sans Mercy*), a text also titled *Jugement de la Belle Dame sans mercy* (Trial of *La Belle Dame sans Mercy*). Achille Caulier denigrates the character in *La Cruelle Femme en amour* (The Woman Cruel in Love). Other texts, anonymous, with telling titles, take her defense: *La Dame loyale en amour* (The Lady Faithful in Love),

La Belle Dame qui eut mercy (The Beautiful Lady Who Had Mercy). The debate continues all the way to Marguerite de Navarre's *Heptameron* (mid-1500s). Excitement surrounded both Chartier's *La Belle Dame sans mercy* and the poet himself, who became a role model because of this "mythical" poem and his political writings, among them the prose *Quadrilogue invectif*. He is praised by Clément Marot, through the character of his father, Jean, in the *Complainte de Monsieur le Général, Guillaume Preudhomme*, as "well spoken in rhyme and prose" (bien disant en rithme et prose). Chartier is also the "father of French eloquence" (*pere de l'eloquence françoyse*) for Pierre Fabri in his *Grant et vray art de plaine rhétorique*, in 1521, and for Jean Bouchet in his *Annales d'Aquitaine* in 1524.

Another sign of these reflections on the literary act is a quarrel that animated the end of the Middle Ages, starting from the classic *Roman de la Rose*. It was begun by Christine de Pizan, backed by Jean Gerson. In opposition were Jean de Montreuil, the provost of Lille, and the secretaries of the king, the Col brothers, Gontier and Pierre, who defended the *Roman*. The debate was simultaneously about the moral of the works, the interpretation of the texts, and the status of the language. As for the moral, Christine singled out shocking passages in the story, such as the saying, "it is better to deceive than to be deceived" (il vaut mieux tromper qu'être trompé). Should the *Roman de la Rose*, or at least certain passages, then be burned? The answer for Christine is yes:

Et le Romant, plaisant aux curieux,
De la Rose, que l'en devroit ardoir!
Mais pour ce mot maint me sauldroit aux yeux
On est souvent batu pour dire voir   (*AUTRES BALLADES*, PIECE 37)

(And the *Romance of the Rose*, which pleases the curious and should be burned! But for saying so many will jump down my throat. One is often beaten for telling the truth.)

Gerson thought likewise. As for the interpretation of the text, the point being debated is the following: who is talking through the mouth of the jealous man and speaking ill of women? For Christine, without hesitation, it is Jean de Meun. The defenders of the *Roman de la Rose* argued their master's innocence, asserting that good criticism should distinguish between author and characters, also Alain Chartier's line of defense in his *Excusation* a few years later, as we have seen. Martin le Franc's *Champion des Dames* likewise testifies to this literary reflection—a new criticism?— on texts.

The final problem stems from the language: could Jean de Meun get away with having Reason pronounce the vulgar word *couilles* (balls; l. 5507), on grounds of the arbitrariness of the signifier, pushing the provocation so far as to say that what Reason refers to here, she could just as well have called "relics"? Christine portrays the impact of the *Roman de la Rose* with much force and humor. She calls on contemporary testimony, in fact, that was brought to her attention by a colleague, Pierre Col: while in a fit of jealousy, a husband had turned to his *Roman de la Rose* and punctuated his reading of its diatribes against women with well-aimed blows to his own wife. The quarrel over the *Roman de la Rose* leads the reader to the heart of an essential problematic: what is literature for? what can it do? For Christine de Pizan, the *Roman de la Rose* does not stand up to comparison with Dante's *Comedy,* as much because of its significance as of its composition and its style. Literary criticism thus becomes international in the Europe of vernacular languages. Who wins, Jean de Meun or Dante?

Ancient and new, antique and modern, the Middle Ages contemplated this dichotomy from the outset and, depending on the time period, mentalities, and temperaments, favored now one pole, now the other. Christianity posed the problematic of the old and the new in both the Old and New Testaments, notably in the parables in Matthew of the old garment and the new cloth (9:16) and the old wineskins and the new wine (9:17).

How was one to come to terms with the past? Antiquity had also bequeathed a legacy to the Middle Ages. How could clerics both revere it and go beyond it? How should the *translatio studii* be perceived? The terms "old" and "new" allow one to note changes in styles.

In music, the expression *nova cantica*, in the twelfth century, distinguishes the new *versus* from the ancient tropes. *L'ars nova* of the fourteenth century goes against the monodic music of the thirteenth century— Guillaume de Machaut speaks of the "vieille et nouvelle forge" (old and new forge).

In poetry, the *Vida* of the troubadour Cercamon says that he "found" "songs and pastourelles in the ancient style" (vers e postoretas a la usanza antiga) while many troubadours claim that they compose *chansoneta nueva*, new words and sounds. Certain texts unite the values of the two poles. *La Vie de sainte Euphrosine* from the beginning of the thirteenth century, claims to sing a "new song from beautiful antiquity" (Nove chançon de bele antiquité), "A new song from ancient times" (Nove chançon del tens ancienor).

In philosophy, as Pierre Michaud-Quantin remarks, "from the thirteenth century, the term *novus* is likely to take on a positive value: thus [a] *translatio nova* is a better translation than those that preceded it."

In the fourteenth century, the *via antiqua* of the realists and the *via moderna* of the nominalists were opposed. There are numerous examples. The designation of the vulgar language had given its name to a genre: the *roman*. Another narrative genre in the second half of the Middle Ages received its signature, no longer from a language, but from an esthetic category: the novella.

Etienne Gilson recalls this in his essay "Le Moyen Âge comme 'Saeculum modernum'": "Nothing was newer in its time than the scholastic method, nothing more modern" (Rien ne fut plus nouveau en son temps que la méthode scolastique, rien de plus moderne). The return to antiquity that characterizes the Renaissance as a historical period was in fact the discovery made by this era of its distance from antiquity. The Middle Ages had converted the gods of antiquity—it was not a question of an anachronism but of a militant act—and the Renaissance returned them to the Pantheon. The Middle Ages turned Latin—and a few other idioms— into French. The Renaissance returned Latin to its culture.

The Middle Ages sang like the birds, wrote without restraint, on any surface, even in Villon on the plaster of the tomb, on the covering of the windows of Philippe Vigneulles' prison; with blood, with ink, with coal.

Prenez en gré; May it please you.

778

Battle of Roncevaux. Death of
Roland.

800

Charlemagne crowned emperor.

842

Two of Charlemagne's grandsons,   First attested use in writing of the
Louis the German and Charles   French and Germanic vernaculars in
the Bald, unite against the third,   the Oaths of Strasbourg.
Lothaire.

End of the ninth century

Séquence de sainte Eulalie (29 lines),
the first known conserved poem in
the French language.

c. 950–1000

Passion by Clermont. *Vie de saint
Léger*

987

Accession of Hugh Capet

1040–1105

Life of Rashi (Solomon, son of
Isaac). He founds a talmudic school
in Troyes [now in Champagne-
Ardenne] that is famous throughout
the Occident

c. 1050

Vie de saint Alexis.

Between 1060 and 1080

Chanson de sainte Foy.

1066

Conquest of England by William,
duke of Normandy. The Battle of
Hastings is celebrated in the embroi-
dery known as the Bayeux Tapestry
(precise date unknown).

1095

Council of Clermont. Preaching
of the First Crusade.

	1099	
Jerusalem falls to the Crusaders.		
	c. 1100	
		The Song of Roland.
	1101	
Foundation of the abbey of Fontevrault by Robert of Arbrissel. Birth of Héloïse.		
	1115	
The future Saint Bernard, then aged 25, founds the abbey of Clairvaux, where he will die in 1153.		
	1118	
Foundation of the order of the Temple (Knights Templar).		
	1127	
Death of William IX, duke of Aquitaine, the "first" troubadour.		
	Between 1130 and 1148	
		Marcabru composes poems.
	c. 1132	
Construction of the Basilica of Saint-Denis begun.		
	1137	
Marriage of Louis VII and Eleanor of Aquitaine.		
	c. 1140–1170	
		The troubadours Bernard de Ventadour, Pierre d'Auvergne, and Raimbaud d'Orange active.
	1142	
Abélard dies.		
	Between 1146 and 1174	
		Le Jeu d'Adam.
	c. 1147	
		Beginning of Bernard de Ventadour's work.
	1151	
Death of Suger, counselor to Louis VII.		
	1152	
Dissolution of Louis VII and Eleanor of Aquitaine's marriage. Eleanor marries Henry Plantagenet. Pierre Lombard, master of the cathedral school of Paris, writes the *Four Books of Sentences.*		

	c. 1152–1154
	Le Roman de Thèbes
	1154
Henry Plantagenet becomes king of England as Henry II.	
	c. 1154–1156
	Le Roman d'Enéas.
	1160
	Marie de France, *Les Lais.*
	1163–1182
Construction of Notre-Dame de Paris.	
	c. 1165
	Benoît de Sainte-Maure, *Le Roman de Troie* (The Romance of Troy).
	Between 1165 and 1200
	Béroul, *Tristan et Iseult.*
	1170
Assassination of Thomas Beckett, archbishop of Canterbury, in his cathedral, prompted by King Henry II.	
	Between 1172 and 1174
	Guernes (Garnier) of Pont-Sainte-Maxence writes his *Vie de saint Thomas Beckett.*
	c. 1175
	First branches of the *Roman de Renart.*
	c. 1180–1200
	Trouvères: Le Châtelain de Coucy, Gace Brulé, and Conon de Béthune.
	1180
Accession of Philip Augustus.	
	c. 1181
	Chrétien de Troyes, *Le Conte du Graal.*
	c. 1185
	Andreas Capellanus, *De amore.*
	1187
Saladin takes Jerusalem.	
	c. 1195
Death of Bernard de Ventadour.	
	1195
Lothar of Segni, the future Pope Innocent III, writes his *De contemptu mundi,* or *De miseria humanae conditionis,* a text conserved in more than six hundred manuscripts.	

	1199	
Death of Richard the Lionheart. John Lackland becomes king of England.		
	c. 1200	
		Jean Bodel, *Jeu de saint Nicolas*.
	1201	
Birth of Theobald of Champagne, grandson of Marie of Champagne, the patroness of Chrétien de Troyes.		
	1203	
Constantinople falls to the Fourth Crusade.		
	1208–1244	
Crusade against the Albigensians ordered by Pope Innocent III to suppress the Cathar heresy.		
	c. 1210	
		Geoffroy de Villehardouin and Robert de Clari write *De la Conquête de Constantinople*.
	1210	
Death of Jean Bodel.		
	1214	
Battle of Bouvines. Philip Augustus defeats the coalition raised against him by John Lackland.		
	1215	
Simon de Montfort, the leader of the Albigensian crusade, becomes count of Toulouse. The Fourth Lateran Council, convoked by Pope Innocent III, ordains annual confession of all adult Christians.		
	c. 1220–1230	
		Gautier de Coincy, *Miracles de Notre Dame*, *Lancelot en prose*. Jean Renart, *Guillaume de Dole*.
	c. 1225	
		Guillaume de Lorris, *Le Roman de la Rose*.
	1225–1230	
		La Queste del Saint Graal.
	1226	
Accession of Louis IX, the future Saint Louis. Regency of Blanche of Castile.		

c. 1238

Death of Pérotin, master of the
Notre Dame school of polyphony,
in Paris.

1245–1248

Construction of the Sainte-Chapelle
in Paris.

1248–1254

Saint Louis leads the Seventh
Crusade.

c. 1250

Strong influence of Averroës (Ibn
Rushd, 1126–1198) at the University
of Paris.

1252–1259

Teaching of Saint Thomas Aquinas
in Paris.

1255

Rutebeuf, *La Discorde des Jacobins
et de l'Université.*

1256

Aldobrandino da Siena, based in
Troyes, writes his *Régime du Corps*
in French, the first medical text in
the vernacular.

1257

Foundation of the Sorbonne.

Rutebeuf writes the *Dit de Maître
Guillaume de Saint-Amour.*

1261

Fall of the Latin Empire of
Constantinople.

Le Mariage Rutebeuf.

1267

Brunet Latin writes *Le Livre du
Trésor* in French.

1270

Death of Saint Louis at Tunis.

1270–1271

Ramon Llull, *Llibre del Gentil e los
tres savis* (Book of the Gentile and
the Three Wise Men).

1271–1295

Marco Polo travels in China.

c. 1275

Jean de Meun continues the *Roman
de la Rose.*

	1276	
		Adam de la Halle, *Le Jeu de la Feuillée*.
	1277	
Stephen Tempier, bishop of Paris, condemns 219 propositions taught at the University of Paris.		
	1285–1314	
Reign of Philip the Fair.		
	c. 1295	
Death of Guiraut Riquier.		
	c. 1300	
Birth of Guillaume de Machaut.		
	1303–1305	
Giotto executes the frescoes of the life of the Virgin Mary and the Christ in the Scrovegni Chapel in Padua.		
	1304	
Birth of Francesco Petrarch. Foundation of the College of Navarre. Among the masters who will direct it: Nicole Oresme, Pierre d'Ailly. Jean Gerson was a student there.		
	1305	
Death of Jean de Meun in Paris.		
	1306	
Expulsion of the Jews by Philip the Fair.		
	1307	
Arrest of the Templars.		Dante begins the *Divine Comedy*.
	1309	
Installation of the papacy in Avignon.		Jean de Joinville, *La Vie de saint Louis*.
	1310–1315	
		Le Roman de Fauvel.
	1313	
Birth of Boccaccio.		
	1314	
Death of Philip the Fair and of Pope Clement V.		
	1316	
Death of Ramon Llull.		
	1328	
Accession of Philip VI of Valois.		

	1334	
Death of Jean Pucelle, illuminator of the *Hours* by Jeanne d'Evreux and of a famous manuscript of the *Miracles of Our Lady* by Gautier de Coincy.		
	1337	
Beginning of the Hundred Years' War.		
	1341	
Petrarch crowned in Rome wearing the purple mantle of the king of Naples.		
	1346	
Battle of Crécy. Defeat of Philip VI by Edward III of England.		Guillaume de Machaut, *Le Jugement du Roi de Bohême*.
	1347–1349	
The Black Death in Western Europe.		Boccaccio, *The Decameron*. Guillaume de Machaut, *Le Jugement du Roi de Navarre*.
	c. 1350	
An anonymous profile portrait of King Jean II of France (Jean le Bon) marks the revival of the individual portraiture of antiquity.		
	1356	
Battle of Poitiers. Defeat of Jean le Bon, who is taken to England as a prisoner. Regency of the Dauphin, the future Charles V.		
	1358	
Revolt and defeat of Etienne Marcel. The Jacquerie.		
	c. 1362–1364	
Guillaume de Machaut composes his polyphonic *Mass*.		
	1363–1365	
		Guillaume de Machaut writes his *Voir Dit*.
	1364	
Accession of Charles V.		
	c. 1365	
Birth of Christine de Pizan in Venice.		
	1369	
		Jean Froissart, *L'Espinette amoureuse*.

	1370
Bertrand du Guesclin is made Constable of France.	
	Between 1370 and 1400
	Jean Froissart writes his *Chronicles*.
	1371
	Le Livre du chevalier de la Tour Landry pour l'enseignement de ses filles.
	1374
Death of Petrarch.	
	1375
Death of Boccaccio.	
	1377
Death of Guillaume de Machaut.	
	Starting in 1377
Apocalypse Tapestry of Angers executed by the Parisian weaver Nicolas Bataille for Louis I of Anjou, brother of Charles V.	
	1378
Beginning of the Great Schism [between the Eastern (Greek) and Western (Latin) branches of the Christian Church].	
	c. 1380
	Geoffrey Chaucer translates the *Roman de la Rose* into English. Jean Froissart composes *Méliador*.
	1380
Death of Charles V. Death of Bertrand du Guesclin.	
	1382
Maillotins Revolt in Paris.	Royal song by Eustache Deschamps with the refrain "Fuiez, fuiez pour les maillès de plonc" (Flee, flee, because of the leaden hammers).
	1383
	Eustache Deschamps writes the *Double Lay de la fragilité humaine*, an adaptation of the *De miseria humanae conditionis* by Lothaire de Segni (1195).
	1387
	Le Livre de la Chasse by Gaston Phoebus, count of Foix.

	1392
Charles VI's first fit of madness.	Eustache Deschamps, *L'Art de dictier.*
	Between 1395 and 1404
Claus Sluter completes his monumental sculpture *The Well of Moses* for the Carthusian monastery of Champmol in Dijon.	
	1396
Turkish victory in the Battle of Nicopolis, with the deaths of Jean le Sénéchal, Philippe d'Artois, and Jean de Crésecque, three of the authors of the *Livres des Cent Ballades.*	
	1399
Richard II of England deposed by Henry of Bolingbroke, who becomes King Henry IV.	
	c. 1400
Birth of the musician Guillaume Dufay in Cambrai.	*Les Quinze Joies de mariage* (The Fifteen Joys of Marriage). Quarrel of the *Roman de la Rose.*
	1401
Writing of *La Cour amoureuse dite de Charles VI.*	
	1404
Death of Philip the Bold.	Christine de Pizan, *Le Livre des fais et bonnes meurs du sage roy Charles V.*
	1405
	Christine de Pizan, *Le Livre de la Cité des Dames.*
	1407
Assassination of Louis of Orléans on the order of the duke of Burgundy John the Fearless. Beginning of the civil war between the Armagnacs, partisans of the assassinated prince, and the Burgundians.	
	c. 1410
Birth of the musician Johannes Ockeghem, for whom Jean Molinet will write a double epitaph, in Latin and French, in 1497.	

1413–1416

The Limbourg brothers create the
Très Riches Heures du duc de Berry.

1414–1418

The Council of Constance criticizes
the papacy.

1415

Battle of Agincourt.
Charles of Orléans is taken prisoner.
He will spend twenty-five years in
captivity in England.

1416

Alain Chartier writes the *Livres des
quatre Dames.*

1418

The Burgundians take control
in Paris. The Dauphin leaves for
Bourges. Alain Chartier, his secretary, accompanies him.

1419

Murder of John the Fearless on the
bridge at Montereau. Philip the
Good succeeds him as duke of
Burgundy.

1420

Treaty of Troyes. The Dauphin,
Charles, is declared a bastard.
Henry V of England is recognized as
heir to the throne of France
when Charles VI dies.

1422

Death of Henry V, then of
Charles VI.

Alain Chartier, *Le Quadrilogue
invectif.*

1424

Alain Chartier, *La Belle Dame sans
Merci.*

1429

Joan of Arc in Chinon.
End of the siege of Orléans.
Coronation and anointment of
Charles VII.

Christine de Pizan writes the *Ditié
de Jeanne d'Arc.*

1431

Joan of Arc is burned alive in
Rouen.

	1435	
Charles VII and Philip the Good, duke of Burgundy, sign the Peace of Arras.		
	1437	
		Charles of Orléans, *La Departie d'Amour*.
	1441	
		Martin le Franc, *Le Champion des Dames*.
	c. 1450	
Johannes Gutenberg's printing press installed in Mainz.		
	c. 1450–1455	
Portrait of Charles VII by Jean Fouquet.		Arnoul Gréban, *Mystère de la Passion*.
	1453	
Constantinople taken by the Turks.		
	1455	
Georges Chastellain becomes *indiciaire*, or official chronicler, of the court of Burgundy.		
	1456	
The duke of Burgundy gives refuge to the Dauphin Louis, the future Louis XI.		François Villon composes *Le Lais*. Antoine de la Sale, *Le Petit Jean de Saintré*.
	Between 1456 and 1469	
		Farce de Maître Pierre Pathelin.
	1457	
		René d'Anjou, *Le Livre du Cuer d'Amours espris*.
	1461	
Death of Charles VII.		François Villon's *Testament*.
	1465	
Death of Charles of Orléans.		
	1467	
Death of Philip the Good. Accession of Charles the Bold.		
	1475	
Georges Chastellain dies. Jean Molinet succeeds him as historiographer to the court of Burgundy.		
	1477	
Battle of Nancy. Death of Charles the Bold.		

1483

Death of Louis XI. Accession of
Charles VIII.

Between 1484 and 1500

Execution of the tapestry pieces of
La Dame à la Licorne.

1489

Death of the painter Simon Mar-
mion, born in 1425. Jean Molinet
writes his epitaph.

1491

Marriage of Charles VIII and Anne
of Brittany.

1492

The Moorish kingdom of Granada
falls to Ferdinand and Isabella of
Spain.
Jews expelled from Spain.
Christopher Columbus reaches
America.

1498–1515

Louis XII is king of France. Josquin
des Prés composes a motet and some
songs for him.

1500

Jean Molinet's *Roman de la Rose,
moralisé.*

NOTES

Introduction

1. A French translation of the article entitled "Le nouveau Moyen Age" can be found in Eco, *Guerre du faux*.

2. Maeterlinck, *Ruysbroeck and the Mystics*, p. 42.

3. Denis Foulechat translated the passage into French in 1372 thus: "Va et, quelque part tu yras, dis que tu es nez de Poitou, car il ont licence de plus franche langue parler."

1. The Materiality of Writing

1. The modern French word *écrivain,* which evolved from *escrivain,* means writer or author.

2. The Question of the Author

1. The French royal chancery consisted of officials, usually clerics, charged with guarding the king's seal and, at times, granting charter rights and other benefits.

2. See pp. 76–77 for analysis.

5. The Subject Matter

1. For a definition of *accessus,* see p. 20.

2. For the rest of this quotation, see p. 39.

3. In Huon le Roi de Cambrai, *Li Regres Nostre Dame.*

4. A sea and a mother, of course, for Gautier: in French, *mer* (sea) and *mère* (mother) are homophones.

6. The Paths to Writing

1. The painting in Codex Vindobonensis 2554, fol. 1, is reproduced in Louis Grodecki, *Le Moyen Age retrouvé,* vol. 2: *De saint Louis à Viollet-le-Duc* (Paris: Flammarion, 1991), p. 22.

9. The Question of Literary Heritage

1. In antiquity, the northwestern coastal region of Gaul of modern Brittany formed what was called "Armorica," the latinization of a Gallic word meaning "the country facing the sea." Jacques Roubaud (b. 1932), is a French poet and mathematician.

BIBLIOGRAPHY

Texts and Authors

Anthologies and Collections

Dufournet, Jean. *Anthologie de la poésie lyrique française des XIIe et XIIIe siècles.* Collection Poésie, 232. Paris: Gallimard, 1989. Old French text with facing modern French translation.

Morawski, Joseph. *Proverbes français antérieurs au XVe siècle.* Les classiques français du Moyen âge [hereafter abbreviated as CFMA], 47. Paris: Champion 1925. Facsimile reprint, 2007.

Eleventh-Century Texts and Authors

La Chanson de Roland. Edited and translated into modern French by Ian Short. Lettres gothiques, 4524. 2nd ed. Paris: Librairie générale française, 1990.

The Song of Roland. Translated into English by Dorothy L. Sayers. Harmondsworth, UK: Penguin Books, 1957.

Twelfth-Century Texts and Authors

Aimon de Varenne. "Le livre du roy flourimont, filz du duc d'Albanye, et de la naissance du roy Philippe, son filz, pere du roy Alexandre le Grant." BNf, fr., MS 12566.

Andreas Capellanus. *De amore.* Translated into modern French by Claude Buridant under the title *Traité de l'amour courtois.* Bibliothèque française et romane, ser. D: Initiation, textes et documents, 9. Paris: Klincksieck, 1974.

Aucassin et Nicolette. Edited and translated by Philippe Walter. Folio classique, 3265. Paris: Gallimard, 1999. Old French text with modern French translation.

Benoît de Sainte-Maure. *Le roman de Troie.* Published from all known manuscripts by Léopold Constans. 6 vols. Société des anciens textes français [hereafter abbreviated as SATF]. Paris: Firmin-Didot, 1904–1912.

———. *Chronique des ducs de Normandie.* Vols. 1–2. Edited by Carin Fahlin. Uppsala, Sweden: Almqvist & Wiksells, 1951–1954.

Bernard de Ventadour. *Chansons d'amour.* Edited by Moshé Lazar. Paris: Klincksieck, 1966.

La Chanson de Guillaume. Edited and translated into modern French by François Suard. Classiques Garnier. Paris: Bordas, 1991.

Chrétien de Troyes. *Arthurian Romances*. Edited and translated by William W. Kibler. *Erec and Enide*, translated by Carleton W. Carroll. London: Penguin Books, 1991.

———. *Romans*. Edited by Charles Méla et al. La Pochothèque. Paris: Librairie générale française, 1994.

Clémence of Barking. *Vie de saint Edouard le Confesseur*. Edited by Östen Södergard. Uppsala, Sweden, 1948.

Conon de Béthune. *Les Chansons*. Edited by Ael Wallensköld. CFMA, 24. Paris: Champion, 1921.

Gace Brulé. *Chansons*. Edited by Holger Petersen Dyggve. Mémoires de la Société néophilologique de Helsinki (Helsingfors), 16. Helsinki: Société néophilologique, 1951.

Gautier d'Arras. *Eracle*. Edited by Guy Raynaud de Lage. CFMA, 102. Paris: Champion, 1976.

Guiraut de Bornelh. *The Cansos and Sirventes of the Troubadour Giraut de Borneil: A Critical Edition*. Edited by Ruth V. Sharman. Cambridge: Cambridge University Press, 1989.

Guernes de Pont-Sainte-Maxence. *Vie de saint Thomas Beckett*. Edited by Emmanuel Walberg. CFMA, 77. Paris: Champion, 1936.

Guillaume IX, duc d'Aquitaine. *Les Chansons de Guillaume IX, duc d'Aquitaine (1071–1127)*. Edited by Alfred Jeanroy. 2nd ed. CFMA, 9. Paris: Champion, [1913] 1927.

Hélinant de Froidmont. *Les Vers de la mort*. Edited by F. Wulff and E. Walberg. SATF. Paris: Firmin-Didot, 1905.

Hildegard von Bingen. *Hildegardis Scivias*. Edited by Adelgundis Führkötter. Corpus christianorum Continuatio mediaevalis, 43, vol. 2. Turnhout, Belgium: Brepols, 1978.

———. *Louanges*. Complete poetry translated into French from Latin and presented by Laurence Moulinier. Orphée. Paris: La Différence, 1990.

Hue de Rotelande. *Ipomedon*. Edited by Anthony J. Holden. Paris: Klincksieck, 1979.

Huon le Roi de Cambrai. *Li Regres Nostre Dame*. Edited by Arthur Långfors. Paris: Champion, 1907.

Jaufré Rudel. *Les Chansons*. Edited by Alfred Jeanroy. 2nd ed. CFMA, 15. Paris: Champion, [1924] 1965.

Jeu d'Adam (Le). (Ordo representacionis Ade). Edited by Willem Noomen. CFMA, 99. Paris: Champion, 1971.

"Liber XXIV philosophorum." *Le Livre des XXIV philosophes: Résurgence d'un texte du IVe siècle,* edited and translated by Françoise Hudry. Paris: J. Vrin, 2009. Latin text with French translation.

Marie de France. *Les Lais.* Edited by Jean Rychner. CFMA, 93. Paris: Champion, 1966.

———. *The Lays of Marie de France.* Translated into English with introduction by Glyn S. Burgess and Keith Busby. London: Penguin Books, 1986.

———. *Lais de Marie de France.* Edited by Karl Warnke. Translated into modern French by Laurence Harf-Lancner. Lettres gothiques, 4523. Paris: Librairie générale française, 1990.

Partonopeu de Blois. Edited and translated into modern French by Olivier Collet and Pierre-Marie Joris. Lettres gothiques, 4569. Paris: Librairie générale française, 2005.

Peire Vidal. *Les Poésies.* Edited by Joseph Anglade. 2nd ed. CFMA, 11. Paris: Champion, 1923.

Philippe de Thaon. *Le Bestiaire.* Edited by Emmanuel Walberg. Paris: H. Welter; Lund, Sweden: H. Möller, 1900.

Piramus, Denis. *La Vie seint Edmund le Rei: Poème anglo-normand du XIIe siècle.* Edited by Hilding Kjellman. Geneva: Slatkine, 1974.

Reclus de Molliens, *Li Romans de Carité* and *Miserere.* Edited by Anton Gerard Van Hamel. 2 vols. Paris: F. Vieweg, 1885.

Robert de Boron. *Merlin and the Grail: Joseph of Arimathea, Merlin, Perceval: The Trilogy of Arthurian Prose Romances attributed to Robert de Boron.* Translated by Nigel Bryant. Cambridge: D. S. Brewer, 2005.

Simon de Freine. *Les Oeuvres de Simund de Freine.* Edited by John Ernst Matzke. SATF. Paris: Firmin-Didot, 1909.

Wace. *Le Romand de Brut.* Edited by Ivor Arnold. 2 vols. Paris: SATF, 1938–1940.

———. *Le Roman de Rou.* Edited by Anthony J. Holden. 2 vols. SATF. Paris: Picard, 1970–1971.

Thirteenth-Century Texts and Authors

Adam de la Halle. *Oeuvres complètes.* Edited by Pierre-Yves Badel. Lettres gothiques, 4543. Paris: Libraire générale française, 1995.

Adenet le Roi. *Les Oeuvres d'Adenet le Roi.* Edited by Albert Henry. Vol. 5, *Cléomadés.* 2 vols. Brussels: Editions de l'université de Bruxelles, 1971.

Alart de Cambrai. *Le Livre de Philosophie et de Moralité.* Edited by Jean-Charles Payen. Paris: Klincksieck, 1970.

Amadas et Ydoine, roman du XIIIe siècle. Edited by John Revell Reinhard. CFMA, 51. Paris: Champion, 1926.

L'Atre périlleux. Roman de la Table Ronde. Edited by Brian Woledge. CFMA, 76. Paris: Champion, 1936.

Bodel, Jean. "Les Congés." In *Les Congés d'Arras (Jean Bodel, Baude Fastoul, Adam de la Halle)*, edited by Pierre Ruelle. Paris: Presses universitaires de France; Brussels: Presses universitaires de Bruxelles, 1965.

———. *La Chanson des Saisnes*. Edited by Annette Brasseur. TLF, 369. 2 vols. Geneva: Droz, 1989.

Brunetto Latini. *Li Livres dou tresor*. Edited by Francis J. Carmody. Vol. 2. University of California Publications in Modern Philology. Berkeley: University of California Press, 1948.

Les Evangiles des Domées. Edited by Robert Bossuat and Guy Raynaud de Lage. Paris: Librairie d'Argences, 1955.

Flamenca. In *Les Troubadours*. Edited and translated into modern French by René Lavaud and René Nelli. Vol. 1. Bibliothèque européenne. 2nd ed. Paris: Desclée, De Brouwer, 1960.

Galeran de Bretagne. Edited under the name of Jean Renart by Lucien Foulet. CFMA, 37. Paris: Champion, 1926.

Gautier de Coincy. *Les Miracles de Nostre Dame par Gautier de Coinci*. Published by Victor Frederic Koenig. 4 vols. Textes littéraires français [hereafter abbreviated as TLF], 64, 95, 131, and 176. Geneva: Droz; Lille: Giard; Paris: Minard, 1955–1970.

Gerbert de Montreuil. *Le Roman de la Violette ou de Gerart de Nevers*. Edited by Douglas Labaree Buffum. Paris: Champion, 1928.

Gervaise. "Le Bestiaire." In *Romania: Recueil trimestriel consacré à l'étude des langues et des littératures romanes*, edited by Paul Meyer, 1: 420–443. Paris: Librairie Franck, 1872.

Girart d'Amiens. *Escanor, roman arthurien en vers de la fin du XIIIᵉ siècle*. Edited by Richard Trachsler. 2 vols. Geneva: Droz, 1994.

Gliglois (Le roman de). Edited by Marie-Luce Chênerie. Paris: Champion, 2003.

Guillaume de Lorris and Jean de Meun. *Le Roman de la Rose*. Edited by Félix Lecoy. 3 vols. CFMA, 92, 95, and 98. Paris: Champion, 1965–1970.

———. *The Romance of the Rose*. Translated into English by Charles Dahlberg. Princeton, NJ: Princeton University Press, 1983.

Henri d'Andeli. *La Querelle des anciens et des modernes au XIIIᵉ siècle, ou la Bataille des VII arts*. Paris: F. Henri, 1875.

———. *Les Dits*. Edited by Alain Corbellari. CFMA, 146. Paris: Champion, 2003.

Herbert. *Le Roman de Dolopathos*. Edited by Jean-Luc Leclanche. 3 vols. CFMA, 124, 125, and 126. Paris: Champion, 1977.

Humbaut. *The Romance of Hunbaut: An Arthurian Poem of the Thirteenth Century*. Edited by Margaret Winters. Leiden: Brill, 1984.

Huon de Mery. *Le Tournoi de l'Antéchrist (Li Tournoiemenz Antecrit)*. Text established by Georg Wimmer. Presented, translated into modern French, and annotated by Stéphanie Orgeur. Orléans: Paradigme, 1994.

Isopets (Recueil général des). Edited by Julia Bastin. SATF. 2 vols. Paris: Champion, 1929–1930.

Jacques de Baisieux. *L'Oeuvre de Jacques de Baisieux*. Edited by Patrick A. Thomas. The Hague: Mouton, 1973.

Jacques de Voragine. *La Légende dorée*. Translated into modern French by Jean-Baptiste Marie Roze. GF 132–133. 2 vols. Paris: Flammarion, 1967.

Jakemes. *Le Roman du Castelain de Couci et de la Dame de Fayel*. Edited by Maurice Delbouille. Paris: SATF, 1936.

Jean de Meung. *Le Roman de la Rose*. See Guillaume de Lorris.

———. *Le Testament Maistre Jehan de Meun*. Edited by Silvia Buzzetti Gallarati. Alessandria, Italy: Edizioni dell'Orso, 1989.

Joinville, Jean de. *Vie de saint Louis*. Edited by Jacques Monfrin. Classiques Garnier. Paris: Dunod, 1995. Reprint. Lettre gothiques, 4565. Paris: Librairie générale française, 2002.

Laurent d'Orléans. *La Somme le roi par Frère Laurent*. Edited by Edith Brayer and Anne-Françoise Leurquin-Labi. Paris: SATF, 2008.

Malkaraume, Jehan. *La Bible de Jehan Malkaraume*. Edited by Jean Robert Smeets. 2 vols. Assen: Van Gorcum, 1977.

Mousket, Philippe. *Chronique rimée*. Edited by Baron Frédéric de Reiffenberg. Brussels: Hayez, 1836–1845.

Philippe de Remi, or de Beaumanoir. *Oeuvres poétiques de Philippe de Remi, sire de Beaumanoir*. Edited by Hermann Suchier. 2 vols. Vol. 1, *La Manekine*, by Philippe de Remi; *Le Roman en prose de la Manekine*, by Jean Wauquelin. Vol. 2, *Jehan et Blonde, Salu d'amours, Conte d'amours, Conte de fole larguece, Fatrasie, Lai d'amours, Ave Maria, Salut à refrains*, three versions of the novella *Gesta romanorum*. SATF. Paris: Firmin-Didot, 1884–1885.

Philippe de Novare. *Les Quatre Ages de l'homme. Traité moral de Philippe de Navarre*. Edited by Marcel de Fréville. SATF. Paris: Firmin-Didot, 1888.

———. *Mémoires, 1218–1243*. Edited by Charles Kohler. CFMA, 10. Paris: Champion, 1913.

Pierre de Beauvais. *Le Bestiaire de Pierre de Beauvais: version courte*. Edited by Guy R. Mermier. Paris: Nizet, 1977.

Pierre de Peckham [Pierre d'Abernon of Fetcham]. *La Lumere as Lais*. Edited by Glynn Hesketh. 3 vols. London: Anglo-Norman Text Society, 1996, 1998, 2000.

Quatre fils Aymon (La chanson des). Edited by Ferdinand Castets. Montpellier: Coulet et fils, 1909.

Quatre fils Aymon (La chanson des). Certain passages translated into modern French by Micheline de Combarieu du Grès and Jean Subrenat. Folio, 1501. Paris: Gallimard, 1983.

Queste du Saint Graal (La). Edited by Fanni Bogdanow. Translated into modern French by Anne Berrie. Lettres gothiques, 4571. Paris: Librairie générale française, 2006.

Raoul de Houdenc. *Le Songe d'Enfer; suivi de La Voie de Paradis*. Edited by Philéas Lebesgue. Paris: E. Sansot, 1908.

——. *Il Roman des Eles di Raoul de Houdenc*. Edited by Matteo Majorano. Bari: Adriatica, 1983.

Renart, Jean. *Le Roman de la Rose ou de Guillaume de Dole*. Edited by Félix Lecoy. CFMA, 91. Paris: Champion, 1962.

Renaut de Beaujeu. *Le Bel Inconnu*. Edited by Michèle Perret. Translated into modern French by Michèle Perret and Isabelle Weill. Champion Classiques. Paris: Champion, 2003.

Richard de Fournival. *La Vieille, ou les Dernières amours d'Ovide*. Translated by Jean le Fèvre. Edited by Hippolyte Cocheris. Paris: Aubry, 1861.

——. *Il bestiario d'amore* and *La risposta al bestiario*. Edited by Fr. Zambon. Biblioteca medievale, 1. Parma: Pratiche, 1987.

Richars li biaus. Roman du XIIIe siècle. Edited by Anthony J. Holden. CFMA, 106. Paris: Champion, 1983.

Romans de Witasse le Moine (Li). Roman du XIIIe siècle. Edited by Denis Joseph Conlon from MS BNF, fr. 1553. Chapel Hill: University of North Carolina Press, 1972.

Rutebeuf. *Oeuvres complètes*. Edited and translated into modern French by Michel Zink. 2 vols. Paris: Bordas, 1989–1990. 1-vol. reprint. Lettres gothiques, 4560. Paris: Librairie générale française, 2001.

Sarrasin. *Le Roman du Hem*. Edited by Albert Henry. Paris: Les Belles Lettres, 1939.

La Suite du Roman de Merlin. Edited by Gilles Roussineau. TLF, 472. 2 vols. Geneva: Droz, 1996.

Thibaut de Champagne. *Les Chansons*. Edited by Axel Wallensköld. SATF. Paris: Champion, 1925.

Tibaut. *Le Roman de la Poire*. Edited by Christiane Marchello-Nizia. Paris: SATF, 1984.

Fourteenth-Century Texts and Authors

Avionnet. In *Recueil général des Isopets*. Edited by Julia Bastin, 349–384. Vol. 2. Paris: SATF, 1930.

Boccaccio, Giovanni. "De mulieribus claris." Edited by Vittore Zaccaria. In *Tutte le opere di Giovanni Boccaccio,* edited by Vittore Branca. Milan: Mondadori, 1967.

———. "De casibus virorum illustrium." Edited by Pier Giorgio Ricci and Vittore Zaccaria. In *Tutte le opere di Giovanni Boccaccio,* edited by Vittore Branca. Milan: Mondadori, 1983.

———. *Decameron* or *Livre des Cent Nouvelles* or *Prince Galeot.* Translated into French by Laurent de Premierfait [1411–1414]. Edited by Giuseppe di Stefano. Montreal: CERES, 1998.

———. *Vie de Dante Alighieri, poète florentin.* Translated into French by Francisque Reynard (1877). Preface by Jacqueline Risset. Marseille: Via Valeriano; Paris: Léo Scheer, 2002.

———. *Le Décaméron.* Translated into French by Giovanni Clerico. Preface by Pierre Laurens. Folio classique, 4352. Paris: Gallimard, 2006.

Chaucer, Geoffrey. *The Works.* Edited by F. N. Robinson. The New Cambridge Edition. 2nd ed. Boston: Houghton Mifflin, 1961.

Christine de Pizan. *Oeuvres poétiques de Christine de Pisan.* Edited by Maurice Roy. SATF. 3 vols. Paris: Firmin Didot, 1886–1896.

———. *Le Livre des fais et bonnes meurs du sage roi Charles V.* Edited by Suzanne Solente. 2 vols. Société de l'histoire de France, 437 and 444. Paris: Champion, 1936–1941.

———. *Le Livre de la Mutacion de Fortune.* Edited by Suzanne Solente. SATF. 4 vols. Paris: Picard, 1959–1966.

———. *Cent Ballades d'Amant et de Dame.* Edited by Jacqueline Cerquiglini [-Toulet]. Bibliothèque médiévale, 10–18; 1529. Paris: Union générale d'éditions, 1982.

———. *La Città delle dame (Le Livre de la cité des dames).* Text in Middle French edited by Earl Jeffrey Richards. Translated into Italian by Patrizia Caraffi. Milan: Luni, 1997.

———. *Le Livre du corps de policie.* Edited by Angus J. Kennedy. Etudes christiniennes, 1. Paris: Champion, 1998.

———. *L'Epistre Othea.* Edited by Gabriella Parussa. TLF, 517. Geneva: Droz, 1999.

———. *Le Chemin de Longue Etude.* Edited and translated into modern French by Andrea Tarnowski. Lettres gothiques, 4558. Paris: Librairie générale française, 2000.

———. *Le Livre de l'advision Cristine.* Edited by Christiane Reno and Liliane Dulac. Etudes christiniennes, 4. Paris: Champion, 2001.

Christine de Pizan, Jean Gerson, Jean de Montreuil, Gontier and Pierre Col. *Le*

Débat sur le "Roman de la Rose." Edited by Eric Hicks. Paris: Champion, 1977. Translated into modern French by Virginie Greene. Traductions des classiques du Moyen Age, 76. Paris: Champion, 2006.

Dante Alighieri. *Oeuvres complètes.* Translated into French by André Pézard. Bibliothèque de la Pléiade. Paris: Gallimard, 1965.

Deschamps, Eustache. *Oeuvres complètes.* Edited by Marquis Auguste de Queux de Sainte-Hilaire and G. Raynaud. SATF. 11 vols. Paris: Firmin Didot, 1878–1903.

Dupin, Jean. *Les Mélancolies.* Edited by Lauri Lindgren. Turku, Finland: Turun Yliopisto, 1965.

Etienne de Conty. "Brevis tractatus." MS, BN, Fonds latin 11730.

Evrart de Conty. *Le Livre des Eschez amoureux moralisés.* Edited by Françoise Guichard-Tesson and Bruno Roy. Montreal: CERES, 1993.

Frayre de Joy et Sor de Plaser. In *Nouvelles courtoises occitanes et françaises.* Edited and translated into modern French by Suzanne Méjean-Thioler and Marie-Françoise Notz-Grob. Lettres gothiques, 4548. Paris: Librairie générale française, 1997.

Froissart, Jean. *Poésies.* Edited by Auguste Scheler. 3 vols. Brussels: Victor Devaux, 1869–1872.

———. *Méliador. Roman comprenant les poésies lyriques de Wenceslas de Bohême, duc de Luxembourg et de Brabant.* Edited by Auguste Longnon. SATF. 3 vols. Paris: Firmin Didot, 1895–1899.

———. *L'Espinette amoureuse.* Edited by Anthime Fourrier. Paris: Klincksieck, 1963. 2nd ed., 1972.

———. *La Prison amoureuse.* Edited by Anthime Fourrier. Bibliothèque française et romane, série B, éditions critiques de textes, 13. Paris: Klincksieck, 1974.

———. *Le Joli Buisson de Jonece.* Edited by Anthime Fourrier. TLF, 222. Geneva: Droz, 1975.

———. *Ballades et rondeaux.* Edited by Rae Suzanne Baudouin. TLF, 252. Geneva: Droz, 1978.

———. *"Dits" et "Débats."* Edited by Anthime Fourrier. TLF, 274. Geneva: Droz, 1979.

———. *Chroniques, Livres I et II.* Edited by Peter F. Ainsworth and George T. Diller. Lettres gothiques, 4556. Paris: Librairie générale française, 2001.

———. *Chroniques, Livres III et IV.* Edited by Peter F. Ainsworth and Alberto Varvaro. Lettres gothiques, 4563. Paris: Librairie générale française, 2004.

Geoffroi de la Tour Landry. *Le Livre du chevalier de la Tour Landry pour l'enseignement de ses filles.* Published by Anatole de Montaiglon. Bibliothèque elzévirienne, 36. Paris: P. Jannet, 1854.

Gilles Li Muisis. *Poésies*. Edited by Baron Kervyn de Lettenhove. 2 vols. Louvain: J. Lefever, 1882.

Guillaume de Digulleville. *Le Pèlerinage de vie humaine de Guillaume de Deguileville*. Edited by Johann Jakob Stürzinger. London: Roxburghe Club, 1893.

Guillaume de Machaut. *La Prise d'Alexandrie, ou Chronique du roi Pierre Ier de Lusignan*. Edited by Louis de Mas Latrie. Publications de la Société de l'Orient latin, série historique, 1. Geneva: J.-G. Fick, 1877.

———. *Oeuvres*. Edited by Ernest Hoepffner. SATF. 3 vols. Paris: Firmin Didot, then Champion, 1908, 1911, 1921.

———. *Poésies lyriques*. Complete edition published by Vladimir Chichmaref. 2 vols. Paris: Champion, 1909. Reprint. 1 vol. Geneva: Slatkine, 1973.

———. "The Dit de la Harpe of Guillaume de Machaut." In *Essays in Honour of Albert Feuillerat*, edited by Karl Young, 1–20. New Haven, CT: Yale University Press, 1943.

———. *La Fontaine amoureuse*. Edited and translated by Jacqueline Cerquiglini-Toulet. Moyen Age. Paris: Stock, 1993.

———. *Le Livre du Voir Dit*. Edited and translated into modern French by Paul Imbs. Introduction and revision by Jacqueline Cerquiglini-Toulet. Lettres gothiques, 4557. Paris: Librairie générale française, 1999.

Honoré Bovet. *L'Apparicion Maistre Jehan de Meun et le Somnium super materia scismatis d'Honoré Bonet*. Edited by Ivor Arnold. Paris: Les Belles Lettres, 1926.

Jacques Legrand. *Archiloge Sophie. Livre de Bonnes Meurs*. Edited by Evencio Beltran. Geneva: Slatkine; Paris: Champion, 1986.

Jacques de Longuyon. *Les Voeux du paon, The Buik of Alexander or the Buik of the most noble and valiant conquerour Alexander the Grit, by John Barbour . . . together with the French originals (Li Fuerres de Gadres and Les Voeux du Paon)*. Edited by R. L. Graeme Ritchie. Scottish Text Society. 4 vols. Edinburgh: W. Blackwood & Sons, 1925–1929.

Jan van Ruusbroec. *L'Ornement des noces spirituelles de Ruysbroeck l'Admirable*. Translated from Flemish by Maurice Maeterlinck. 1891. Facsimile reprint. Brussels: Les Eperonniers, 1990.

Jean d'Arras. *Mélusine* or *La noble histoire de Lusignan*. Edited and translated into modern French by Jean-Jacques Vincensini. Lettres gothiques, 4566. Paris: Librairie générale française, 2003.

Jean de Brie. *Le Bon Berger, ou le vray régime et gouvernement des Bergers et Bergères, réimprimé sur l'édition de Paris (1541)*. Edited by Paul Lacroix. Paris: Isidore Liseux, 1879.

Jean de Condé. *Dits et contes de Baudouin de Condé et de son fils Jean de Condé*.

Edited by Auguste Scheler. Vols. 2–3, *Jean de Condé*. Brussels: Victor Devaux, 1866–1867.

———. *La Messe des oiseaux* and *Le Dit des jaconbins et des Fremeneurs*. Edited by Jacques Ribard. TLF, 170. Geneva: Droz, 1970.

Jean de Garencières. *Le Chevalier Poète Jehan de Garencières (1372–1415). Sa vie et ses poésies complètes dont de nombreuses inédites*. Edited by Young Abernathy Neal. Paris: Nizet, 1953.

Jean de le Motte. *Li Regret Guillaume, Comte de Hainaut. Poëme inédit du XIVᵉ siècle*. Edited by Auguste Scheler. Louvain: J. Lefever, 1882.

———. *La Voie d'Enfer et de Paradis: An Unpublished Poem of the Fourteenth Century by Jehan de le Mote*. Edited by Sister M. Aquiline Pety. Washington, DC: Catholic University of America Press, 1940.

———. *Le Parfait du Paon*. Edited by Richard J. Carey. Chapel Hill: University of North Carolina Press, 1972.

Jean Maillart. *Le Roman du Comte d'Anjou*. Edited by Mario Roques. CFMA, 67. Paris: Champion, 1931. Translated into modern French by Francine Mora-Lebrun. Folio classique 3087. Paris: Gallimard, 1998.

Jean le Seneschal. *Les Cent Ballades, poème du XIVᵉ siècle composé par Jean le Seneschal avec la collaboration de Philippe d'Artois, comte d'Eu, de Boucicaut le Jeune et de Jean de Crésecque*. Published by Gaston Raynaud. SATF. Paris: Firmin Didot, 1905.

John of Salisbury. *Tyrans, princes et prêtres (Jean de Salisbury, Policratique IV et VIII)*. Edited by Charles Brucker. Montreal: CERES, *Le Moyen Français 21*, 1987.

———. *Le Policratique de Jean de Salisbury (1372)*. Books 1–3. Translated by Denis Foulechat. Edited by Charles Brucker. Publications romanes et françaises 209. Geneva: Droz, 1994.

———. *Le Policratique de Jean de Salisbury (1372)*. Book 5. Critical edition of the French and Latin texts with commentary and translation by Charles Brucker. Publications romanes et françaises 242. Geneva: Droz, 2006.

La manière de langage qui enseigne à bien parler et écrire le français. Modèles de conversation composés en Angleterre à la fin du XIVᵉ siècle. Edited by Jean Gessler. Brussels: Edition universelle; Paris: Droz, 1934.

Le Court, Jean. *Le Restor du paon. Jean Le Court dit Brisebare*. Critical edition by Richard J. Carey. TLF, 119. Geneva: Droz, 1966.

Le Fèvre, Jean. *Les Lamentations de Matheolus* and *Le Livre de Leesce de Jehan Le Fèvre, de Ressons*. Edited by Anton Gerard Van Hamel. Bibliothèque de l'Ecole des hautes études, série Sciences historiques et philologiques, 96. Vol. 2. Paris: E. Bouillon, 1895.

————. *Le Respit de la Mort*. Edited by Geneviève Hasenohr-Esnos. SATF. Paris: Picard, 1969.

Le Mesnagier de Paris. Edited by Georgina E. Brereton and Janet M. Ferrier. Translated into modern French by Karin Ueltschi. Lettres gothiques, 4540. Paris: Librairie générale française, 1994.

Nicole Oresme. *Le livre de Ethiques d'Aristote*. Edited by A. D. Menut. New York: Stechert, 1940. Published from Bibliothèque royale de Belgique MS 2902.

Oton de Grandson. *Sa vie et ses poésies*. Edited by Arthur Piaget. Lausanne: Payot, 1941.

Ovide moralisé, poème du commencement du XIVᵉ siècle. Edited by C. de Boer et al. Verhandelingen der Koninklijke Nederlandsche Akademie van Wetenschappen, Afdeeling Letterkunde, n.s., 15, 21, 30/3, 37, and 43. 5 vols. Amsterdam: J. Müller, then N. V. Noord-Hollandsche Uitgevers-Maatschappij, 1915–1938.

Petrarch (Francesco Petrarca). *Oeuvres*. Published under the direction of Pierre Laurens. Les Classiques de l'Humanisme. Paris: Les Belles Lettres, 2002–.

Philippe de Mézières. *Le Songe du Vieil Pelerin*. 2 vols. Edited by George W. Coopland. Cambridge: Cambridge University Press, 1969.

Renart le Contrefait (Le Roman de). Edited by Gaston Raynaud and Henri Lemaître. 2 vols. Paris: Champion, 1914.

Le Songe du Vergier. Edited by Marion Schnerb-Lièvre. 2 vols. Paris: Centre national de la recherche scientifique, 1982.

Le Tombel de Chartrose (Dix-huit contes français tirés du reccueil intitulé). Edited by Ewald Kooiman. Amsterdam: Graduate Press, 1975.

Le Trésor amoureux. Edited by Auguste Scheler. In *Oeuvres de Froissart*, vol. 3: *Poésies*. Brussels: Victor Devaux, 1872.

Watriquet de Couvin. *Dits de Watriquet de Couvin*. Edited by Auguste Scheler. Brussels: Victor Devaux, 1868.

Fifteenth-Century Texts and Authors

Adevineaux amoureux, Les. *Amorous Games: A Critical Edition*. Edited by James Woodrow Hassell Jr. Publications of the American Folklore Society, Bibliographical and Special Series, 25. Austin: University of Texas Press, 1974.

Alexis, Guillaume. *Oeuvres poétiques*. 3 vols. Edited by Arthur Piaget and Emile Picot. SATF. Paris: Firmin Didot, 1896–1908.

Antitus. *Poésies*. Edited by Manuela Python. TLF, 422. Geneva: Droz, 1992.

"L'Art et science de rhétorique." Anonymous. In *Récueil d'arts de seconde rhétorique*, edited by Ernest Langlois. 1902. Facsimile reprint. Geneva: Slatkine, 1974.

Baudouin, Jean. "Un Manuscrit autographe de L'Instruction de la vie mortelle." In *Romania: Recueil trimestriel consacré à l'étude des langues et des littératures romanes*, edited by G. Hasenohr, 104: 257–260. Paris, 1983.

Blosseville. "Le Débat du Vieil et du Jeune." In *Une nouvelle collection de poésies lyriques et courtoises du XVᵉ siècle. Le manuscrit B.N. Nouv. Acq. Fr. 15771.* Edited by Barbara L. S. Inglis, 174–186. Paris: Champion, 1985.

Bugnin, Jacques de. *Le Congié pris du siecle seculier. Poème du XVᵉ siècle.* Edited by Arthur Piaget. Recueil des travaux publiés par la Faculté des lettres de l'Académie de Neuchâtel, 6. Neuchâtel, Attinger, 1916.

Les Cent Nouvelles Nouvelles. Edited by Franklin P. Sweetser. TLF, 127. Geneva: Droz, 1966.

Chartier, Alain. *Le Quadrilogue invectif.* Edited by Eugénie Droz. 2nd ed. CFMA, 32. Paris: Champion, 1950.

———. *The Poetical Works of Alain Chartier.* Edited by James Cameron Laidlaw. Cambridge: Cambridge University Press, 1974.

———. *Le Livres de l'Esperance.* Text established by François Rouy. Bibliothèque du XVᵉ siècle, 51. Paris: Champion, 1989.

Chartier, Alain, Baudet Herenc, and Achille Caulier. *Le Cycle de "La Belle Dame sans mercy."* Bilingual Middle French–modern French edition by David F. Hult, with the collaboration of Joan E. McRae. Champion classiques, série Moyen Age, 8. Paris: Champion, 2003.

Chastellain, Georges. *Oeuvres.* Edited by Joseph Kervyn de Lettenhove. 8 vols. Brussels: Heussner, 1863–1866. Reprint. Geneva: Slatkine, 1971. Vols. 1–2: *Chronique: 1419–1422; Chronique: 1430–1431, 1452–1453.*

———. *Le Temple de Bocace.* Edited by Susanna Bliggenstorfer. Bern: Francke, coll. Romanica Helvetica 104, 1988.

Commynes, Philippe de. *Mémoires.* Edited by Joël Blanchard with the collaboration of Michel Quereuil. Lettres gothiques, 4564. Paris: Librairie générale française, 2001.

La Cour amoureuse dite de Charles VI. Edited by Carla Bozzolo and Hélène Loyau. Paris: Le Léopard d'Or, 1982.

Crétin, Guillaume. *Oeuvres poétiques de Guillaume Crétin.* Edited by Kathleen Chesney. Paris: Firmin Didot, 1932.

De Metz, Guillebert. *Description de la ville de Paris au XVᵉ siècle.* Edited by Antoine Le Roux de Lincy. Paris: Aubry, 1855.

Garin, François. *Les Complaintes et enseignemens de Françoys Guérin, marchant de Lyon, envoyées à son filz.* Paris: Guillaume Mignart, 1495.

Gerson, Jean. *Le "Donat espirituel" de Colard Mansion: étude et édition.* Edited by Maria Colombo Timelli. Milan: Istituto lombardo di scienze e lettere, 1997.

Gréban, Arnoul. *Le Mystère de la Passion.* Edited by Omer Jodogne. Mémoires de l'Académie royale de Belgique, Classe des Lettres, 2nd ser., 12.3. 2 vols. Brussels: Palais des académies, 1965–1983.

Hauteville, Pierre de. *La Confession et testament de l'amant trespassé de deuil.* Edited by Rose M. Bidler. Inedita & Rara, 1. Montreal: CERES, 1982.

———. *La Complainte de l'amant trespassé de dueil. L'inventaire des biens demourez du decés de l'amant trespassé de dueil.* Edited by Rose M. Bidler. Le Moyen Français, 18. Montreal: CERES, 1986.

La Chesnaye, Nicolas de. *La Condamnation de Banquet.* Edited by Jelle Koopmans and Paul Verhuyck. TLF, 395. Geneva: Droz, 1991.

La Haye, Olivier de. *Poème sur la grande peste de 1348 publié d'après le manuscrit de la bibliothèque du Palais Sainte-Pierre.* Edited by Georges Guigue. Lyon: H. Georg, 1888.

La Marche, Olivier de. *Mémoires d'Olivier de La Marche, maître d'hôtel et capitaine des gardes de Charles le Téméraire.* Published for the Société de l'histoire de France by Henri Beaune and Jules d'Arbaumont. 4 vols. Paris: Renouard, 1883–1888.

———. *Le Triumphe des Dames.* Edited by Julia Kalbfleisch. Rostock: Adler's Erben, 1901.

La Sale, Antoine de. *Oeuvres complètes.* Edited by Fernand Desonay. Vol. 1: *La Salade;* vol. 2: *La Sale.* Bibliothèque de la Faculté de philosophie et lettres de l'Université de Liège, 68, 92. Paris: Droz, 1935, 1941.

———. *Jehan de Saintré.* Edited by Joël Blanchard. Translated into modern French by Michel Quereuil. Lettres gothiques, 4544. Paris: Librairie générale française, 1995.

Le Franc, Martin. *Le Champion des Dames.* 5 vols. Edited by Robert Deschaux. CFMA, 127–131. Paris: Champion, 1999. Book 4 edited and translated by Steven Millen Taylor under the title *The Trial of Womankind: A Rhyming Translation of Book IV of the Fifteenth-Century Le Champion des dames* (Jefferson, NC: McFarland, 2005).

Martial d'Auvergne. *Les Arrêts d'amour de Martial d'Auvergne.* Edited by Jean Rychner. SATF. Paris: Picard, 1951.

Meschinot, Jean. *Les Lunettes des Princes.* Edited by Christiane Martineau-Génieys. Publications romanes et françaises, 121. Geneva: Droz, 1972.

Michault, Pierre. *Le Doctrinal du Temps Present* (1466). Edited by Thomas Walton. Paris: Droz, 1932.

Le Mistère du Vieil Testament. Edited by James de Rothschild. SATF. 6 vols. Paris: Firmin Didot, 1878–1891.

Molinet, Jean. "Chant Royal." In *Récueil d'arts de seconde rhétorique,* edited by Ernest Langlois. Paris: Impr. nationale, 1902.

———. *Les Faictz et Dictz de Jean Molinet*. Edited by Noël Dupire. SATF. 3 vols. Paris: Société des anciens textes français, 1936–1939.

Orléans, Charles d'. *Poésies*. Edited by Pierre Champion. CFMA, 34 and 56. 2 vols. Paris: Champion, 1923, 1927.

———. *Ballades et rondeaux*. Edited by Jean-Claude Mühlethaler. Lettres gothiques, 4531. Paris: Librairie générale française, 1992.

Pathelin, Pierre. "Le Testament de Pathelin." In *La Trilogie de Pathelin*, edited and translated by Françoise Morvan. Arles: Actes Sud, 2009.

Regnier, Jean. *Les Fortunes et adversitez*. Edited by Eugénie Droz. SATF. Paris: Champion, 1923.

René I, duc d'Anjou. *Le Livre du coeur d'amour épris*. Edited and translated into modern French by Florence Bouchet. Lettres gothiques, 4567. Paris: Librairie générale française, 2003.

Robertet, Jean. *Oeuvres*. Edited by Margaret Zsuppán. Geneva: Droz, 1970.

Saint-Gelais, Octovien de (attributed to). *La Chasse d'amours. Poème publié en 1509*. Edited by Mary Beth Winn. TLF, 322. Geneva: Droz, 1984.

———. *Le Séjour d'honneur*. Edited by Frédéric Duval. TLF, 545. Geneva: Droz, 2002.

Taillevent, Michault. *Un Poète bourguignon du XVᵉ siècle: Michault Taillevent*. Edited by Robert Deschaux. Publications romanes et françaises, 132. Geneva: Droz, 1975.

Vigneulles, Philippe de. "Poésies inédites, 1491," edited by Verdun-Louis Saulnier, and "Philippe de Vigneulles rimeur de fêtes, de saints et de prisons." In *Mélanges . . . offerts à Charles Rostaing*, 2: 965–991. Liège: Association des romanistes de l'Université de Liège, 1974.

Villon, François. *Poésies complètes*. Edited by Claude Thiry. Lettres gothiques, 4530. Paris: Librairie générale française, 1991.

Wauquelin, Jean. *La Belle Hélène de Constantinople*. Edited by Marie-Claude de Crécy. TLF, 547. Geneva: Droz, 2002. A prose version of a chanson de geste.

Sixteenth-Century Texts and Authors

Bouchet, Jean. *Les Annales d'Aquitaine*. Poitiers: Monnin, 1524.

Champier, Symphorien. *La Nef des dames vertueuses*. Lyon: 1502, 1503. Paris: 1515, 1531.

Du Four, Antoine. *Les Vies des femmes célèbres*. Edited by Gustave Jeanneau. TLF, 168. Geneva: Droz, 1970.

Fabri, Pierre. *Le Grant et vray art de pleine rhétorique*. Edited by A. Héron. 3 vols. Rouen: Société des bibliophiles normands, 1889–1890.

Gascoigne, George. "Certaynes notes of Instruction concerning the making of verse or ryme in English." 1575. In *The Complete Works of George Gascoigne*

. . .: *The posies*, edited by John W. Cunliffe. Cambridge: Cambridge University Press, 1907.

Lemaire de Belges, Jean. *Oeuvres*. Vol. 1. *Les Illustrations de Gaule et Singularitez de Troye*. Edited by J.-A. Stecher. 1882. Facsimile reprint. Geneva: Slatkine, 1969.

Marot, Clément. *Oeuvres poétiques*. Edited by Gérard Defaux. Classiques Garnier. 2 vols. Paris: Bordas, 1990, 1993.

Montaigne, Michel de. *Les Essais*. Edited by Jean Balsamo, Michel Magnien, and Catherine Magnien-Simonin. Bibliothèque de la Pléiade. Paris: Gallimard, 2007.

Sébillet, Thomas. *Art poétique français*. In *Traités de poétique et de rhétorique de la Renaissance*, edited by Francis Goyet. Le Livre de poche. Paris: Librairie générale française, 1990.

Tory, Geofroy. *Champ Fleury, ou l'Art et science de la proportion des lettres*. Paris, 1529. Facsimile reprints: edited by Gustave Cohen (Paris: Bosse, 1931); edited by Kurt Reichenberger and Theodor Berchem (Geneva: Slatkine, 1973).

Studies

Adorno, Theodor Wiesengrund. "On the Use of Foreign Words." In *Notes to Literature*, edited by Ralph Tiedemann, translated by Shierry Weber Nicholsen, 2: 286–291. New York: Columbia University Press, 1992.

Belting, Hans. *Bild und Kult: Eine Geschichte des Bildes vor dem Zeitalter der Kunst*. Munich: C. H. Beck, 1990. Translated by Edmund Jephcott as *Likeness and Presence: A History of the Image Before the Era of Art* (Chicago: University of Chicago Press, 1994), and by Frank Müller as *Image et culte. Une histoire de l'art avant l'époque de l'art* (Paris: Cerf, 1998).

Borges, Jorge Luis. "La Esfera de Pascal." In *Otras inquisiciones*. Madrid: Alianza, 1952.

Bulatkin, Eleanor Webster. "The Arithmetic Structure of the Old French *Vie de Saint-Alexis*." *PMLA* 74 (1959): 495–502.

Cerquiglini-Toulet, Jacqueline. *La Couleur de la mélancolie. La fréquentation des livres au XIVᵉ siècle (1300–1415)*. Paris: Hatier, 1993.

———. *Guillaume de Machaut et l'écriture au XIVᵉ siècle: "Un engin si soutil."* Bibliothèque du XVᵉ siècle, 47. Paris: Champion, 1985, 2001.

Chaytor, Henry J. *From Script to Print: An Introduction to Medieval Vernacular Literature*. Cambridge: W. Heffer & Sons, 1966.

Cheyette, Fredric L. *Ermengard of Narbonne and the World of the Troubadours*. Ithaca, NY: Cornell University Press, 2001.

Crapelet, G.-A., ed. *Proverbes et dictons populaires: avec les dits du mercier et des marchands, et les crieries de Paris, aux XIIIᵉ et XIVᵉ siècles*. Facsimile reprint. *Anciens monuments de l'histoire et de la langue françaises*, 7. Geneva: Slatkine, 1976.

Curtius, Ernst Robert. *Europäische Literatur und lateinisches Mittelalter*. 1948. Translated into French by Jean Bréjoux under the title *La Littérature européenne et le Moyen Age latin*. Paris: Presses universitaires de France, 1956, 1986.

De Bruyne, Edgar. *Etudes d'esthétique médiévale*. 1946. New ed. Bibliothèque de l'Evolution de l'humanité. 2 vols. Paris: Albin Michel, 1998.

Eco, Umberto. *La Guerre du faux*. Translated into French by Myriam Tanant with the collaboration of Piero Caracciolo. Paris: Grasset, 1985. Reprint. Librairie générale française, 1987.

Foucault, Michel. "Qu'est-ce qu'un auteur?" *Bulletin de la société française de philosophie* 64 (1969): 73–104. In id., *Dits et écrits, 1954–1988*, edited by Daniel Defert and François Ewald, vol. 1: *(1954–1969)*, 789–821. Bibliothèque des Sciences humaines. Paris: Gallimard, 1994.

Gilson, Etienne. "Le Moyen Age comme 'Saeculum modernum.'" In *Concetto, storia, miti e immagini del Medio Evo*, 1–10. Edited by V. Branca. Venice: Sansoni, 1973.

Histoire de la langue et de la littérature française des origines à 1900. Edited by Louis Petit de Julleville. 8 vols. Paris: Armand Colin, 1896.

Huizinga, Johan. *Herfsttij der Middeleeuwen: Studie over levens- en gedachtenvormen der veertiende en vijftiende eeuw in Frankrijk en de Nederlanden*. Haarlem: H. D. Tjeenk Willink, 1919. Translated into French by Julia Bastin as *L'Automne du Moyen Age* (1932); new ed. with preface by Jacques Le Goff (Paris: Payot, 1980). Translated by Fritz Hopman as *The Waning of the Middle Ages: A Study of Forms of Life, Thought, and Art in France and the Netherlands in the Dawn of the Renaissance* (London: E. Arnold, 1924).

Jauss, Hans Robert. "Littérature médiévale et théorie des genres." *Poétique* 1 (1970): 79–101.

———. "Littérature médiévale et expérience esthétique. Actualité des *Questions de littérature* de Robert Guiette." Translated into French from German by Michel Zink. *Poétique* 31 (1977): 322–336.

Långfors, Arthur. *Les Incipit des poèmes français antérieurs au XVIe siècle. Répertoire bibliographique établi à l'aide de notes de M. Paul Meyer*. Paris: Champion, 1917.

Lanson, Gustave. *Histoire de la littérature française*. Paris: Hachette, 1895.

Le Goff, Jacques. *Pour un autre Moyen Age. Temps, travail et culture en Occident. 18 essais*. Bibliothèque des histoires. Paris: Gallimard, 1977.

———. *La Naissance du Purgatoire*. Bibliothèque des histoires. Paris: Gallimard, 1981.

Lehmann, Paul. *Parodie im Mittelalter*. Munich: Drei Masken, 1922.

Lewis, Clive S. *Studies in Words*. Cambridge: Cambridge University Press, 1960, 1967.

Maeterlinck, Maurice. *Ruysbroeck and the Mystics: with Selections from Ruysbroeck*. Translated by Jane T. Stoddart. London: Hodder & Stoughton, 1894.

Martin, Henri-Jean, and Roger Chartier, dir. *Histoire de l'édition française*. Vol. 1. *Le Livre conquérant. Du Moyen Age au milieu du XVIIᵉ siècle*. Paris: Promodis, 1982.

Michaud-Quantin, Pierre. *Etudes sur le vocabulaire philosophique du Moyen Age*. Rome: Edizioni dell'Ateneo, 1970.

Paris, Gaston, and Langlois, Ernest, eds. *Chrestomathie du moyen âge, extraits publiés avec des traductions, des notes, une introduction grammaticale et des notices littéraires*. Paris: Hachette, 1897.

Panofsky, Erwin. *Gothic Architecture and Scholasticism*. Latrobe, PA: Archabbey Publications, 2005.

Proverbes et dictons populaires: avec les dits du mercier et des marchands, et les crieries de Paris, aux XIIIᵉ et XIVᵉ siècles. Edited by G.-A. Crapelet. Facsimile reprint. Anciens monuments de l'histoire et de la langue françaises, 7. Geneva: Slatkine, 1976.

Roy, Bruno, ed. *L'Art d'amours. Traduction et commentaire de l'*Ars amatoria d'Ovide. Leiden: E. J. Brill, 1974.

Segre, Cesare. "La Structure de la *Chanson de sainte Foy*." In *Mélanges de langue et de littérature du Moyen Age et de la Renaissance offerts à Jean Frappier*, vol. 1. Geneva: Droz, 1970.

Sharman, Ruth V, ed. *The Cansos and Sirventes of the Troubadour Giraut de Borneil: A Critical Edition*. Cambridge: Cambridge University Press, 1989.

Stock, Brian. *Listening for the Text: On the Uses of the Past*. Baltimore: Johns Hopkins University Press, 1990.

Vinaver, Eugène. *A la recherche d'une poétique médiévale*. Paris: Nizet, 1970.

Yates, Frances A. *The Art of Memory*. Chicago: University of Chicago Press, 1966.

Zink, Michel. *Poésie et conversion au Moyen Age*. Paris: Presses universitaires de France, 2003.

Zumthor, Paul. *Parler du Moyen Age*. Paris: Minuit, 1980.

———. *La lettre et la voix. De la "littérature" médiévale*. Paris: Seuil, 1987.